The *Expanded DBT Skills Training Manual* offers an enriched
robust nature of this form of treatment, little emphasis is place ....
or labels. Instead, Dr. Pederson has well illustrated that DBT is a mindset and skill set to
alleviate human suffering and improve our general effectiveness in leading meaningful lives.
The book gives both therapists and clients worksheets to make the otherwise complicated
DBT approach accessible to everyone who can profit from it. It shows the interaction of the
different skills modules to problem resolution, rather than simply listing each module as if it
stands on its own. Clearly written and easy to understand, this book should be an excellent
resource to all DBT clients and therapists.

Thomas Marra, Ph.D.
President, Center for DBT

There is an urgent need within the mental health field to create practical, coherent and cost-
effective treatment models that reflect the complexity of the problems we treat. There is an
equally urgent need among our clients to learn skills that actually help them feel better, and
that they can continue to develop outside of the therapist's office. Lane Pederson and Cortney
Sidwell Pederson bring these two streams together in this sophisticated training manual that
is at once both simple and intricate. They offer a wide range of specific, teachable skills in
the form of worksheets, exercises and activities that make a fine contribution to the growing
field of Dialectical Behavior Therapy.

Henry Emmons, MD
Author of *The Chemistry of Joy: A Three Step Program*
for Overcoming Depression Through Western Science
and *Eastern Wisdom and The Chemistry of Calm: A Powerful,*
Drug-Free Plan to Quiet Your Fears and Overcome Your Anxiety

This text is the most comprehensive DBT resource available to date. It will prove useful to
both the experienced DBT clinician and therapist new to this model. It can also serve as a
resource to clients looking to integrate DBT into their daily lives. This resource has taken
the evidence based foundations of DBT and expanded and extended the usefulness of this
model through new ideas, suggestions and clinical tools.

Cathy Moonshine, PhD, MSCP, MAC, CADC III
Author of *Dialectical Behavior Therapy Volumes I, II*

This book is jam packed with new and creative information for both facilitators of DBT
and those looking for self help that really delivers. The Pedersons bring their extensive
experience in helping folks through the roughest spots of life to expand and improve the
already effective DBT model.

Barry L. Duncan,
Author, *On Becoming a Better Therapist*

THE EXPANDED DIALECTICAL BEHAVIOR THERAPY SKILLS TRAINING MANUAL

Practical DBT for Self-Help, and Individual and Group Treatment Settings

by

LANE PEDERSON,
PSYD, LP, DBTC

with

CORTNEY SIDWELL PEDERSON,
MSW, LICSW, DBTC

- Expanded explanations for the classic modules
- Expanded examples and application worksheets
- Five *new* skills modules for therapists and clients
- Teaching strategies and skills to overcome barriers
- Explanations of clinical policies and program forms
- Can be used across settings and diagnoses or as a *self-help* book

Copyright © 2012 by Lane Pederson
Published by
Premier Publishing and Media
CMI Education Institute, Inc
3839 White Ave
Eau Claire, WI 54703

Printed in the United States of America

ISBN: 978-1-936128-12-9

Library of Congress Cataloging-in-Publication Data

Pederson, Lane.

The expanded DBT skills training manual : for self-help and individual

and group therapy settings / Lane Pederson, with Cortney Sidwell Pederson.

p. cm.

Includes bibliographical references.

ISBN-13: 978-1-936128-12-9 (pbk.)

ISBN-10: 1-936128-12-8 (pbk.)

1. Dialectical behavior therapy. I. Pederson, Cortney Sidwell. II. Title.

RC489.B4P43 2011

616.89'142--dc23

2011049236

To our children,
Sophie and Sawyer

Contents

About The Authors

Lane Pederson, PsyD, LP, DBTC, is the founder and CEO of Dialectical Behavior Therapy National Certification and Accreditation Association (DBTNCAA), the first active organization to certify DBT providers and accredit DBT programs.

Dr. Pederson co-owns Mental Health Systems, PC (MHS), one of the largest DBT-specialized practices in the Midwest United States with multiple locations. Additionally, MHS is a training center for psychology and social work graduate students and interns as well as post-doctoral fellows. At MHS, Dr. Pederson has developed DBT programs for adolescents and adults, has served as a clinical and training director, and has overseen the care of thousands of clients with co-morbid Axis I and II disorders in intensive outpatient settings. Moreover, he has coordinated and directed clinical outcome studies.

Dr. Pederson is a highly-rated and in-demand international speaker and educator in DBT and personality disorders. He has also presented on self-injurious behaviors, treatment-resistant clients, and dissociative identity disorder with a common emphasis on practical approaches to complex client situations. He has a particular interest in evidence-based practices and advocating for "what works" with clients. He has provided consultation to therapists, teams, case management agencies, and mental health clinics.

Cortney Sidwell Pederson, MSW, LICSW, DBTC, is a DBT therapist who has designed and implemented custom DBT programs. She has worked with adolescents and adults in multiple settings across levels of care. She also participates in the ongoing training and supervision of DBT therapists at MHS.

The authors live in Minnesota with their two children and three dogs.

Preface

Our work with DBT began in 1999 at a nonprofit community mental health center. Back then, DBT was just starting to disseminate into the mental health field as an exciting and promising treatment for clients with borderline personality disorder.

The DBT program developed in that setting had a group format based on a day treatment model and level of care. This program treated some of the highest-risk clients in Minneapolis, Saint Paul, and the surrounding areas and developed a reputation for effective work with difficult client problems.

Our DBT team was active, involved, motivated, and idealistic. We studied and discussed the work of Dr. Marsha Linehan (the developer of DBT) and made it our own, always looking to our clients for information on how to improve the program. We wanted to provide the best possible service, and we cared passionately about the program and clients.

As our DBT program developed, we consulted constantly and pushed each other to be more effective therapists. Our approach embodied the evidence-based practice defined by the American Psychological Association (APA) many years later.

Many of the therapists from this DBT day treatment program went on to develop successful DBT programs in other clinics or in their own practices over the next decade.

DBT as an approach is now at an interesting crossroads. A brief discussion of standard (Linehan) versus other models of DBT and evidence-based practice is included in this book because of the "adherence" movement (i.e. the mandate that DBT therapists need to strictly follow the standard model) promoted by Dr. Linehan and her training company Behavioral Tech, LLC.

The framework and protocols of the standard model provide an effective approach for many providers and programs. For others, the adherence movement represents an undialectical regression in practice that fails to address the needs of clients across settings and levels of care. The standard model works, but not for all clients in all settings. One size does not fit all.

What does the evidence say? In the forest of psychotherapy outcome research, Linehan's studies represent eight overvalued trees. As stated in the APA-published book *The Heart and Soul of Change,*

To be frank, any assertion for the superiority of special treatments for specific disorders should be regarded, at best, as misplaced enthusiasm, far removed from the best interests of consumers.

(Miller et al., 2010, p. 422)

The jury has been in for some time. The evidence is clear that adherence to particular treatment manuals and the use of "specific ingredients" in therapy account for little change, whereas the application of a credible approach in the context of therapeutic factors (i.e., common factors) results in robust change (Duncan et al, 2010; Wampold, 2001).

We encourage DBT providers and programs to follow the evidence, especially the clinical outcomes you monitor in your own settings with your own clients. Trust the teachings, not the teacher, and remember that a Buddhist attitude fits the facts.

Dr. Linehan's contribution to the field has been immense, and she is a true pioneer. At the same time, the knowledge that constitutes DBT resides in the public domain, just like the core approaches that Dr. Linehan adapted to develop this wonderful theoretical orientation.

It may well be time for DBT to transcend its developer to reach the many diverse clients who can benefit from it across frameworks and settings, creating a "second wave" in DBT.

We wish you the best in your application of the skills in this book to your clients in your setting, DBT or otherwise.

Acknowledgments

Thank you to Claire Zelasko, Mike Olson, and Mike Conner. We appreciate your ongoing support and the integrity you bring to PESI's pursuit to bring knowledge to people. We also thank Linda Jackson and Kayla Omtvedt, for your care, patience, and hard work on this manual.

Special acknowledgement goes to everyone at Mental Health Systems, PC (MHS), especially Shelley Furer and Mark Carlson. We appreciate your friendship and your encouragement of the many ideas and ventures that happen within and outside of MHS. The staff and therapists at MHS are first rate, and we appreciate the opportunities we have to work alongside talented, committed, and fun people. Finally, much gratitude goes to past, current, and future clients who constitute the best teachers and the greatest inspiration. Thank you for your immeasurable contributions.

About DBT Programs and Therapists: A Brief Introduction

DBT stands for Dialectical Behavior Therapy. It was developed by Dr. Marsha Linehan to treat people who have chronic suicidal thinking and behaviors as well as other behaviors that disrupt their lives. The specific population that Dr. Linehan studied while developing DBT was women with Borderline Personality Disorder (BPD).

Today, we know that DBT can be used across clinical settings for a variety of problems (Dimeff & Koerner, 2007; Marra, 2005; Moonshine, 2008) and that the skills and approach can be used proactively in health and growth models, too.

DBT is an approach that is both highly innovative and highly derivative (dialectically speaking). In her development of DBT, Linehan was wise to choose from ideas and interventions that already had substantial research and practice to support their use.

In her landmark book, *Cognitive-Behavioral Treatment of Borderline Personality Disorder*, Linehan (1993a) wrote:

> *The strategies used in this and the following chapters no doubt have many things in common with aspects of the other varieties of psychotherapy currently in use ... In writing this original draft of this volume, I read every other treatment manual I could find, both behavioral and nonbehavioral. I also read books that tell new therapists how they are supposed to behave in therapy. Whenever I found a treatment component or strategy that was the same or similar to one used in DBT, I tried to use similar language to describe it. Thus, in a sense, much of this manual has been 'stolen' from preceding manuals. (p. 200)*

In therapy, few ideas are completely new and novel, but really committing to and emphasizing helpful concepts can be hugely effective. One established concept that Linehan commits to and emphasizes is that we need to learn skills to replace behaviors that do not work and to address problems that cause difficulties in how we function in life.

Teaching skills is essential to DBT. Skills can be taught in either individual or group settings (or both), and they are the central focus of this book.

In addition to skills training, DBT emphasizes an accepting, nonjudgmental, and validating approach to clients. This approach means that DBT therapists work hard to understand their clients' world and acknowledge how clients' feelings, thoughts, and behaviors make sense given the context of their unique situation.

This validation is balanced with change strategies. Often, therapists will use validation to open up clients to try something different with skills and behaviors. The DBT change strategies follow traditional behaviorism closely but also include cognitive, psychodynamic, and client-centered interventions, among others. Although purists may disagree, DBT approximates a technically eclectic approach.

Supplementing this great variety of change strategies, DBT incorporates the Eastern concepts of mindfulness and the philosophical underpinnings of dialectics.

DBT therapists use Diary Cards (forms for clients to track symptoms, feelings, and skills) in sessions to determine the priorities for treatment and chain analysis (called *Change Analysis* in this book) to highlight options and help clients learn. Additionally, they address safety issues and anything that interferes with treatment (e.g., lateness, absences, nonparticipation) before any other issues.

DBT therapists may be available by phone to coach clients between appointments and actively seek consultation from other therapists on the treatment team or other professionals. Consultation helps therapists stay motivated and effective.

Note that some therapists may not be DBT-oriented but may follow another approach and/or integrate approaches along with teaching skills from this and other sources. It is fine for therapists to use different approaches; the key is whether the approach works for their clients. Therapists and clients can address the therapist's approach during a discussion on informed consent to treatment.

Some DBT therapists might only see clients individually, and other DBT therapists might see clients in comprehensive programs. "How much" DBT clients need depends on their unique requirements and the level of care indicated. As a general rule, if clients have ongoing safety issues or are chronically unstable, they will probably do best in a structured DBT program.

Professional opinions vary about whether structured DBT programs should follow Linehan's original treatment model ("standard" DBT). Research is clear that "adherence" to treatment models (i.e., how closely therapists follow the protocols of a treatment model) has no effect on clinical outcomes (Webb, 2010), so not all programs have to follow the standard model exactly.

Linehan's research has primarily compared the standard model to treatment as usual (TAU), a control condition that is more like a placebo than another bona fide treatment model. In 2007, Clarkin and colleagues compared DBT to other treatment models and found no differential efficacy. Their conclusion was that "structured treatments work for Borderline Personality Disorder." This news is positive for clients, because having a variety of treatment options is beneficial.

Standard DBT is an approach that helps many people, but the full body of psychotherapy outcome research does not support that DBT needs to follow this model. In fact, customizing a DBT program is an evidence-based practice.

The Evidence-Based Practice of Psychology (EBPP), as defined by the American Psychological Association (APA), recognizes that researched models are not directly applicable to all real-world clients, so changes based on therapists' expertise guided by clients' culture, characteristics, and preferences are frequently indicated (2005). Just as different treatment models are beneficial, a variety of established DBT models are, too. In other words, "one size does not fit all." The monitoring of clinical outcomes and adjusting treatment based on that information is also an essential part of evidence-based practice.

In the real world, DBT programs are developed to meet the needs of unique clients seen in unique settings because clients can be different in important ways from research subjects (e.g., differences in gender, ethnicity, diagnosis, and level of care needed). The approach should be customized to the client. The standard model and other applications of DBT are both valid; the effectiveness of one over another depends on the needs of the clients served. In most cases, supportive programs and therapists with clear structure, rules, and expectations will be most helpful.

Clients choosing a DBT program or therapist should be sure to ask about how clinical outcomes (data showing how effective the treatment is) are monitored and used to adjust the therapy approach for clients and to make overall program improvements.

Overall, the therapeutic factors of "good" DBT (and other treatments for BPD) will include clear structure, rules, and expectations; a dialectical balance of validation and change; and an accepting, respectful, and active therapist who supports *and* challenges clients (Weinberg et al., 2011). These factors, applied through active and collaborative alliances between clients and therapists with agreed-upon goals, will strongly predict positive change (Wampold, 2001).

About this Book: An Orientation for Therapists

As mentioned previously, the teaching of skills is essential to DBT. This book almost exclusively focuses on skills and their application to help people build satisfying lives.

We refer readers interested in full explanations of DBT theory, philosophy, and interventions to Linehan's (1993a) excellent (and essential) book, Thomas Marra's (2005) *DBT in Private Practice*, and Cathy Moonshine's (2008) *Acquiring Competency and Achieving Proficiency with Dialectical Behavior Therapy, Vol. I, The Clinician's Guidebook*.

Linehan's (1993b) original skills manual, *Skills Training Manual for Borderline Personality Disorder*, includes "Mindfulness," "Distress Tolerance," "Emotion Regulation," and "Interpersonal Effectiveness" modules. This book approaches the skills in these classic modules with a fresh perspective, expanded explanations, and new examples and applications. New skills have been added to these modules on occasion, and original acronyms have been changed sometimes. Readers who use different manuals and books will notice the differences and can choose what to teach or apply based on personal preference.

Modules, skills, and acronyms from Linehan are clearly cited in the "Source Citations for Modules and Skills" section near the end of the book. This section includes Linehan's skills along with the present authors' expanded skills. Note that other authors, such as Marra (2004) and Moonshine (2008), have also expanded and customized DBT skills. Readers are referred to their works for their contributions.

In addition to the classic modules, this book expands into five other modules:

Dialectics: Absent from Linehan's manual, the Dialectics Module teaches clients how to find the middle path with thinking and behaviors. Like with mindfulness, learning dialectics can be complicated, but the concepts are enormously helpful when understood and applied.

Problem-solving: Clients often try to solve problems through emotion mind or through haphazard, trial-and-error approaches that are not grounded in values. The Problem-solving Module teaches clients how to define problems and options and to take action guided by their priorities, goals, and values.

Building a Satisfying Life: Research shows the importance of structure, and this module teaches clients how to structure a satisfying life with ongoing and balanced routines.

Boundaries: Often called "limits" in standard DBT, the Boundaries Module teaches clients how to observe, develop, and maintain boundaries to stay safe and build and maintain healthy relationships.

Shifting Thoughts: Linehan (1993a) has noted her objections to more formal cognitive interventions and rationalized their near absence from the standard DBT approach. The current authors take a dialectical view on cognitive interventions grounded in DBT philosophy. This module teaches clients how to observe and shift thinking without invalidating feelings.

To be manageable to therapists and clients, this book contains enough text to explain the concepts but hopefully not so much as to overwhelm the reader or compromise the book's direct usefulness in therapy. You may notice a fair amount of repetition in concepts; the repetition and overlap are by design so that central ideas can be over-learned. Effective ideas can take on a mantra-like presence in time, orienting clients toward skill use.

The section on "Teaching DBT Skills," and the section on "Clinical Policies, Contingencies, and Related Forms" primarily address therapists (although clients could read these sections if interested; a demystified approach can be beneficial to clients).

Clients can typically start with the "Learning DBT Skills" section for a basic orientation and then work through the book.

Teaching DBT Skills

DIFFERENT METHODS

Skills can be taught to individuals, groups, or both. Mindfulness is traditionally taught first (although Dialectics is first in this book), and its main points are repeated in subsequent modules. Most programs and therapists have a rolling curriculum.

Many therapists wonder if skills need to be taught in order or sequence. They also wonder how much time should be dedicated to each skill or module. Cookie cutter answers bring cookie cutter results, so be flexible enough to customize skills training to your clients' needs. Dialectically, you should approach skills teaching with a plan that takes into account the needs and energy of the individual or group. Sometimes you may go through a skill quickly or simply review it, and at other times you may spend a long time on a skill if it is particularly interesting or relevant to the needs of the individual or group.

Therapists may also choose to insert a skill from another module if it helps clients make connections, revisit a skill spontaneously if it is needed, or even bring in a completely novel skill from another source. In individual therapy, skills most relevant to current difficulties can be taught.

The modules in this book and the skills in the modules are laid out in a suggested order. However, they are deliberately not numbered so that therapists can adapt the order as needed.

Teaching out of Linehan's manual for many years, both authors found an individualized "flow" to presenting the skills that did not always follow the original design. The key is balancing a structured and predictable approach with sufficient flexibility.

Many programs wait for the start of a module (e.g., Mindfulness) before new clients are allowed to begin a program. We believe this can be a mistake. Clients will pick up the skills eventually, and we believe it is more important to start clients who need therapy as soon as possible than to wait for an arbitrary time.

If you are an individual therapist who comes from another theoretical orientation, you can simply use this book as a resource to pick and choose skills for clients as needed.

While many therapists may be acquainted with the following teaching methods, it is also true that we often default to the style that is familiar to us. In DBT, we ask clients to practice difficult and unfamiliar skills. Our professional growth (which results in benefits to clients) comes from our practice of different teaching approaches. Practice the ones that feel unfamiliar and awkward (and use those feelings to understand your clients' feelings as they learn and practice skills!).

Interactive Lecture: Present the topics and verbally expand on the written explanations and examples. Expect your clients to participate. Have participants take turns reading the material with back and forth discussion, questions, answers, and the sharing of viewpoints.

Take time to think about and discuss the concepts in the skills teaching, sometimes going line by line to make sure connections are being made and the material is being understood. Many of the concepts are simple and complex at the same time.

Discuss your participation expectations with your clients and leave time and space for them to think about the topics and formulate responses. Do not instantly jump in to fill silence or dominate the lecture.

Socratic Questioning: Socratic questioning is a method that draws clients to answer their own questions. You can question assumptions, views, reasons, consequences, and the questions themselves. This process helps clients to think critically and own the resulting conclusions. Socratic questioning is dialectical in nature, in that the questions move clients to conclusions that may exist on a different "place" on the dialectic.

Group Presentation and Discussion: In group therapy, assign skills or sections of skills to each client to teach the others. Assigning skills to dyads or triads also works well. Not only do clients integrate the skills through teaching, but this approach also challenges clients to practice Distress Tolerance and Interpersonal Effectiveness among other skills.

In-Group Experiential Learning: Experiential learning has clients practice skills in session with support, feedback, and coaching. Experiential learning also exposes clients to barriers so problem-solving can occur.

Be creative with your ideas to make the skills real and behaviorally based for clients. Using arts and crafts can be a great way to learn and practice skills.

Beginning and ending sessions with mindfulness is a wonderful example of experiential learning.

Role-Plays: Role-plays are a specialized type of experiential learning that can be used to work on interpersonal skills. Clients (and therapists) often need to use Nonjudgmental Stance to engage in role-plays.

Frequent role-plays become part of the norm in therapy. Make role-plays relevant but have fun with them, too.

Modeling: Role-plays are effective partly due to modeling. Remember that nearly every interaction is an opportunity to model skills. Also point out when peers or others are modeling a skill and be sure to name it. Modeling is a powerful form of learning, as captured in the idiom, "Monkey see, monkey do." Be sure to reinforce desired new behaviors.

Mix in Audio, Video, and Other Media: Make skills relevant by connecting to songs, movies, and other media that hold your clients' attention and interest. These connections explain concepts in unexpected ways. Be on the lookout for opportunities to use these stimulating tools to position skills. Adolescents especially enjoy this approach to teaching skills.

Behavioral Homework: Homework focused on practicing skills is essential to effective outcomes. Orient clients to the idea of homework and explain why it is important. (Or better yet, use Socratic questioning to get to that conclusion!)

Clients become desensitized to homework when it is assigned each session and is part of the therapy milieu. Be sure to follow up on assignments and treat resistance and lack of follow-through as therapy-interfering behavior (TIB). Homework should be individualized to each client's unique problems and opportunities and relevant to his or her treatment goals and objectives.

ADDRESSING BARRIERS WHILE DEVELOPING SKILLS

Make it Client Driven: Barriers develop when clients do not connect skills teaching to their priorities, goals, and values. Therapists must explicitly help clients see how each skill relates to their Life Vision and what they want from therapy.

When clients can connect to the "why," they can overcome barriers to figure out the "how" with skills. Continually show clients the "carrot" that matters to them.

Identify Stuck Points: Use behavior change analysis to figure out where clients get stuck and then use Socratic questioning to have clients decide how different skills might make a difference.

Recognize What Worked: Clients (and therapists) often think about skills in terms of success and failure. Dialectically, something about a skill has probably been effective on some level. Therapists must recognize the effective part of efforts to shape and reinforce behaviors. When clients receive reinforcement for the part of a behavior that was effective, they are more likely to be open to coaching and correcting the ineffective part(s).

Prescribe the Missing Skill: Clients need to "use skills to use skills." Often Mindfulness is the missing skill. Use your greater knowledge of the connections between skills to direct clients when they cannot find the missing skill or skills themselves. This approach works well when balanced with the previous two approaches.

Catch and Label Skill Use: Therapists get caught addressing deficits rather than building strengths. Therapists consult on how to address problem behaviors and sometimes neglect the other end of the dialectic. Instead of attending to the problem, it is frequently more effective to be ready to reinforce the behaviors (skills) that exist in the absence of problem behaviors.

Clients rarely emit problem behaviors continuously, and all clients continuously engage in skills without awareness (theirs and ours). Actively use Observe and Describe to recognize skills in action and label them to so they can be used with intention next time.

"Coach Up" Clients' Efforts: Great coaches can inspire their players to give maximal effort, which can lead them to perform seemingly beyond their abilities. This phenomenon highlights the power of belief and expectancy, which trumps therapy model in clinical outcomes (Duncan et al., 2010). Be a great coach.

Reinforce Efforts and Accomplishments: Clients will increase efforts and practice more skills when reinforced. Continuous reinforcement establishes new behaviors, and intermittent reinforcement maintains them. Once a client starts to perform a skill, the behavior must be maintained or it will diminish and may be unintentionally extinguished.

Therapists overlook opportunities to reinforce, especially when they get too focused on deficits. When we extinguish old behaviors, we need to reinforce replacement skills. Make sure clients' support systems and environments reinforce skill use (and avoid punishing it), too.

Remember that clients engage in many more positive than negative behaviors. Noticing and reinforcing positive behaviors that happen in the absence of problem behaviors is essential when working to help clients change.

OTHER TIPS

Here are some additional tips for skills teaching. One is to create a manual for clients and ask them to bring it to session. As skills are taught, expect clients to take notes and recap the teaching. Include your clinical policies and rules in the manual.

Another technique is to use a whiteboard to write down key words and make diagrams as you explain skills. Clients benefit from augmenting our words with visuals. A whiteboard can be used in individual sessions, too, and sometimes during clients' processing and problem-solving time.

Have posters or other visuals with the skills on the walls. Allow clients to design posters for their group room to create bonding and ownership.

Sit in on other therapists' skills teaching to pick up fresh ideas, and dedicate some consultation time to "talking skills." Therapists new to DBT can have difficulty with the concepts, and experienced DBT therapists can become unimaginative in their teaching. New and tenured therapists can help each other by working together.

Remember that skills manuals do not need to be treated as all-inclusive. Expand on the skills with your own knowledge, examples and related material from a variety of sources; including materials from other sources helps keep skills training fresh and interesting for therapists and clients.

Finally, use clients' wisdom in skills teaching. Create space for clients to participate and educate each other (and you!).

Learning DBT Skills

AN ORIENTATION FOR CLIENTS

DBT skills are life skills. Many people have said they wish these skills had been taught to them in school. A lot of people never had the opportunity to learn skills and perhaps did not have parents or anyone else model a skillful approach to life.

If we do not see examples of skills being used, it is more difficult to learn them. As the skills are studied, be on the lookout for instances in which you might see skill use around you by others. Actively learn through seeking connections and through practice. Practice makes you prepared to use skills successfully in your life.

Learning DBT skills is like learning a new language. Try to encourage yourself to minimize frustration. Skills you might not have learned yet will be referenced as you study other skills. This cross-referencing is deliberate so over time you can see the connections between skills and how they work together.

When we learn languages, the words have limited meaning and effect until they are put in sentences and then in conversations. The skills work the same way. Keep connecting skills to other skills until they form chains of new behaviors, creating a more satisfying life. We learn a language through speaking it; we need to practice skill use everyday until it is fluent.

Many of the skills' names are referred to by their abbreviations (e.g., Opposite to Emotion is often called "O2E") in practice. The abbreviations for skills will follow the name of the skill in main headings. These connections will help you associate the names with the abbreviations.

For example, a skill such as Wise Mind is abbreviated as WM, so it will appear as Wise Mind (WM) in the heading for the section about the teaching of this skill. You can also reference the "Master Skills List" to see skills' names, abbreviations, and brief explanations.

All of the teachings and applications have a "core concept" identified. This idea will orient you to a primary function or purpose behind the skill. As you study and practice each skill, try and see how the core concept might relate to your priorities, goals, and values. If you can make a connection, it will help to motivate you to continue refining that skill until it is a part of your life. Also remember that learning skills requires daily review and practice.

Work on creating your satisfying life one step at a time, one day at a time. We all have setbacks. These setbacks and problems can be opportunities to learn and grow.

Before jumping in, it helps to outline your Life Vision on the following page. Your Life Vision will help guide you through the skills and keep your journey on track.

Do not give up. There are many people like you on similar journeys. Keep moving and stay open to influencing and being influenced by your world.

My Life Vision (LV)

Core concept: Knowing "why" you want change moves you toward change.

A vision for your life helps to define your priorities, goals, and values, and the roads you want to explore on your journey. Fill in each section of this worksheet and refer to it often. Do not judge what you write down: It is your vision based on your wants, needs, and dreams. You will start with a big picture and then fill in smaller details. Imagine you are painting a picture of the life you can work toward.

Look to revise the picture every few months as you grow and improve. We are all works in progress, so changes will happen. Use the information from this exercise for treatment planning with your therapist.

It is difficult for some people to imagine a satisfying life, especially when they feel hopeless and out of options. If this is your situation, fill in what you can today and do not judge yourself for struggling with this exercise. As you learn skills over time, your Life Vision will come into focus.

LIFE VISION: BIG PICTURE APPLICATION

Describe your priorities, goals, and values in life. What is important to you? What is your motivation to improve? How would you like life to be different? What would/will you be doing if you managed life more effectively? What are your dreams in life?

Describe what you do effectively and what you want to improve on in each of the following areas. See how what you do and what you want to improve on will be part of the Big Picture. Remember that even small details can impact your Life Vision in important ways. Create one manageable goal for each area that builds on what you do effectively or that addresses a desired improvement.

Mental Health:

Physical Health:

Chemical Health (avoiding drugs and alcohol):

Education (school or self-education):

Work or projects:

Volunteering or contributions:

Financial:

Home environment:

Leisure:

Family:

Friends:

Spirit (religion or other connection):

Choose one to three of your goals in these areas to get started on, and refer to them often.

Describe your strengths and other resources that will help you move toward your goal(s):

Describe how your life will be different when you accomplish your goal(s):

Describe how you will acknowledge and celebrate your accomplishment(s):

Dialectics

Core concept: Find balance and walk the middle path.

We sometimes miss the middle ground options between opposites or extremes. There are many ways to look at the same situation and many ways to solve the same problem, but emotions can lead to black and white thoughts and actions. When we get stuck in extremes, we add needless suffering to our emotional pain. A way out is to "work the dialectic."

What does it mean to work the dialectic? First, we notice that life is full of conflicts between wants and needs and countless other dilemmas. These conflicts happen within us, between us, and all around us continuously, and they require our ongoing attention to be effective in resolving them.

When these conflicts and problems appear to be "black and white" to us and others, it can be hard to see the middle options that could create an effective change. We overlook the "grays" between the black and the white.

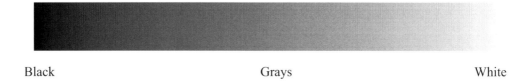

Black   Grays   White

Moving into the grays to create options for change takes a certain mindset. With dialectics, we look for the relative truth in both the black and the white, knowing that opposites can both contain elements of truth at the same time. To find what is valid, it is important to look at the context of each extreme.

When we see the context of each extreme, we also see how they are connected and compliment each other. For example, night and day exist as opposites yet are connected and complement each other. Both are necessary, and there are gradations between midnight and noon.

Another example is the two conflicting proverbs "Birds of a feather flock together" and "Opposites attract." Both proverbs have truth to them even though they exist 180 degrees apart. Which saying better represents how we choose relationships? It depends, and in reality most of the people in our lives have both similarities and differences from us. Each proverb has its own truth and validity.

Remember that truth and validity are relative to the unique context and demands of each situation and to "what works." Considering how difficult or problem behaviors might be adaptive, functional, or somehow work is one way to discover and validate relative truth. How do these behaviors meet emotional, psychological, relational, or other wants and needs? Extremes that do not seem to make sense for us (and others) when we do not see the context actually *do* make sense for us (and others) when we understand how we (or others) are meeting needs through these extremes; this is dialectic and is what we want to validate.

Note that an extreme may make sense put into its context *and* might be grossly ineffective at the same time. For example, people often seek changes in life when behaviors get too problematic and no longer meet needs as effectively or when the consequences of those behaviors become too great. So even when those behaviors meet valid needs, it is also true that changes in the opposite direction may be indicated. Validating both sides of the dialectic helps to create movement toward an effective change.

This movement usually, though not always, requires some balance and synthesis to be effective. Too much movement in one direction may create the need for the opposite, but that does not mean we need to flip to the other extreme!

So when we validate the *context* of each side of our dialectical *conflicts*, then we can open ourselves up to balanced and effective *change*. This is working the dialectic.

Confusing? The following pages will shed more light on dialectics.

Dialectics Applied to Other Skills

Core concept: Dialectics are central to DBT skills.

We can apply the concept of dialectics to many of the skills and concepts learned in DBT. Even when dialectics are not explicitly mentioned, it may be useful to see if they apply. Note examples of dialectics in the descriptions of other skills; for example, the balance of emotion and reason to find Wise Mind is a dialectic. (see Mindfulness)

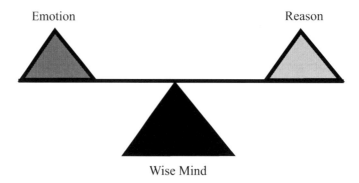

It is common for our emotions and our reason to conflict, and how emotional versus how reasonable to be in a situation depends on what works. When we go too far in one direction—way into emotion mind or way into reasonable mind—the need for the opposite is created.

To resolve the conflict, we validate each opposite based on the context of the situation. Our emotions make sense, as does reason. Finding the balance is what brings us to Wise Mind, that centered place where we respect our emotions *and* make effective choices.

Using both GIVE and DEAR MAN with others is another dialectical example. (see Interpersonal Effectiveness)

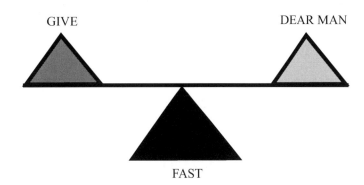

We must remain mindful to the balance between others' wants and needs (GIVE) and our wants and needs (DEAR MAN) in relationships. If we get too focused on others or ourselves, we need to find balance to resolve the conflict based on the context and needs of each interaction. Often we use our FAST skills, in particular our values, to guide how we strike balances in relationships.

In Distress Tolerance, we can choose between mindfulness versus distraction when in distress. Alternatively, we may decide between attending to a problem versus distracting from it. Both of these examples illustrate dialectics.

Pros and Cons are also a dialectical exercise. The nature of Pros and Cons highlights how choices can have both an upside and a downside that need consideration when you are trying to resolve conflicts or solve problems.

Try to notice how dialectics apply to different skills and related concepts as you work through this book.

Using MIDDLE Cs (MC)

Core concept: We orient ourselves to the middle to work the dialectic.

Use the acronym *MIDDLE Cs* to remember the building blocks (**M**indful of Black and White; **I**dentify Shades of Gray in Thoughts, Behaviors, Relationships, and Situations; **D**on't Get Stuck; **D**o Allow Shifts; **L**ive a Life with Options; **E**xtremes Rarely Work; **C**s: Bring Context to Conflict to Create Change) of this skill. These building blocks are described in further detail in the paragraphs that follow.

Mindful of Black and White: Is an extreme happening with emotions, thoughts, behaviors, relationships, or situations? Use Observe and Describe to nonjudgmentally define the extreme(s) and then the opposite end of the dialectic. Find the "truth" in each end and validate how it makes sense given the context.

Identify Shades of Gray in Thoughts, Behaviors, Relationships, and Situations: Work to actively find the middle ground options. Wise Mind helps. So does consulting with others you trust. Try to determine the effectiveness of each option with the current conflict. A mix of curiosity and understanding facilitate this process.

Don't Get Stuck: Minimize willfulness and alternating between extremes. Observation of being "stuck" indicates that a conflict exists. Remember that an extreme contains the seed of its opposite, signaling a need for balance.

Do Allow Shifts: Maximize Willingness. Remember that dialectics mean working out of "either/or" to create balance and meet the demands of the situation.

Live a Life with Options: Life is hard when we feel trapped and without choices. "Living in the grays" can be scary at first because it is less familiar than black and white. Ultimately, middle choices lead to a more balanced and satisfying life. Find ways to create effective compromises in dialectical conflicts.

Extremes Rarely Work: Sometimes an extreme is effective, but usually it is not. Choose an extreme only when it fits priorities, goals, and values and the needs of the situation as viewed from Wise Mind.

Cs: Bring Context to Conflict to Create Change: Change happens when we understand and validate each end of a dialectic conflict while recognizing its context. Then, a dialectic shift may happen. Remember that change requires movement ... in thought and action!

MIDDLE Cs AND COMMON DIALECTICAL CONFLICTS

Core concept: See shades of gray in dialectical conflicts.

Following are common examples of dialectical conflicts. For each conflict, practice the skill MIDDLE Cs to validate the opposites and identify middle options. You can write any notes here or on a separate sheet of paper. If a conflict does not seem to apply to your life, imagine how it might in a different situation or for a different person.

Self-acceptance versus change:

Wanting a different life while resisting change:

Being the real you versus being vulnerable to others:

Structure versus freedom:

Novelty versus predictability:

Fears of needing people conflicting with fears of being independent:

Desire to succeed while actively destroying your progress:

Setting goals that are too easy or goals that are too hard:

Caring for others and still maintaining boundaries:

Balance of self versus others:

Letting go of control to gain control:

Seeing only pros or only cons of a situation:

Not being a doormat and not being demanding:

Asserting your values while respecting the values of others:

Finding the middle between passive and aggressive:

Both being capable and asking for help:

Being too private versus being an open book:

Doing your best and needing to do better:

Balance of "old" self with "new" self:

"Want-tos" versus "have-tos":

Taking a situation personally when it is not about you:

Wanting perfection and knowing you are human:

An all-or-nothing approach to anything:

Picking your battles:

MIDDLE Cs LIFE EXAMPLES

Core concept: Ideas to bring dialectics to everyday life.

Think about how each example may apply to your present situation or life and how to create balanced thought and action. You can write any notes here or on a separate sheet of paper.

Make small changes in diet or exercise:

Play the "devils advocate" (gently):

Acknowledge another person's point of view (does not require agreement):

Accept feedback you would rather reject:

Resist being "right":

Balance new thinking with old beliefs:

Validate someone when you feel angry toward him/her:

Take the middle ground:

Negotiate or compromise:

Practice a new behavior or skill that doesn't feel like you:

Give yourself credit for success:

Notice that you or others are not all "good" or "bad":

See how opposite action may help you, and then practice it:

Delay action when you feel reactive:

"Burn the bridge" to ineffective behaviors:

Take action when you feel passive:

Evaluate your values when they are in conflict, and make a choice:

Seek to understand rather than impose judgment on self, others, and/or situations:

Find the meaning or the "silver lining" in a terrible situation:

Be open to the facts of the situation in spite of strong feelings:

Allow your feelings even when they do not fit the facts:

Activate Wise Mind:

MIDDLE Cs APPLICATION ONE

Core concept: Use this worksheet to practice MIDDLE Cs.

Describe opposites or extremes in your life:

Describe what is valid or gained from each extreme position:

Describe the opposite viewpoints and what is valid or gained from them:

Describe how you can find AND practice middle ground options:

Describe how your life will be different when you practice middle ground options:

Describe how you will acknowledge and celebrate walking the middle path:

MIDDLE Cs APPLICATION TWO

Core concept: Use this worksheet when stuck in a dialectical conflict.

Describe your conflict (be specific):

Describe the other skills you need to be dialectical (e.g., Wise Mind, Nonjudgmental Stance, FAST, GIVE, DEAR MAN):

Describe your current "place" on the dialectic and how it makes sense (find the context and validate it!):

Describe the opposite (or another) position and how it makes sense (find the context and validate it!):

Describe the balance or synthesis of both positions and how this dialectic makes sense:

Describe your specific dialectical action plan (your movement toward change!):

Describe how your life will be different when you resolve this conflict:

Describe how you will acknowledge and celebrate the resolution of this conflict:

Mindfulness

Core concept: Mindfulness is the gateway to an effective and enjoyable life.

Mindfulness is the foundation of DBT skills. It allows us to gain awareness of our feelings, thoughts, behaviors, relationships, and environment. Awareness then helps us to make more informed and effective choices and build a more satisfying life. Neuroscience research shows that mindfulness makes positive and lasting changes to our brains.

Central to mindfulness is the concept of taking hold of one's mind. This means concentrating our attention on what we choose rather than having emotions, thoughts, or other experiences control us. Training yourself to collect, unify, and direct your attention creates containment in your mind.

Mindfulness skills open doors to acceptance, experience, and connection to yourself and the world. This approach is additive and allows for more complete and richer information and experience to guide us. It is also different from some of our default ways of being: disconnected, judgmental, and alone. These default approaches reduce our experience because we label and categorize and quickly move on without viewing the bigger picture.

As we learn mindfulness, we want to remember that it needs to be practiced with other skills and nurtured. The concepts behind mindfulness can be straightforward, but being mindful in our lives requires attention and disciplined practice over time. Like most worthwhile pursuits, our efforts dedicated to mindfulness will reap great benefits if practiced daily.

The Mindfulness Module teaches us the core skills to get us to Wise Mind. From Wise Mind, we can live centered and balanced lives using both our hearts and minds and stay one-mindful in the present, visiting the past and future by choice and connecting with ourselves and the world in a nonjudgmental fashion. Ultimately, we use mindfulness to slow down and find peace, contentment, and enjoyment in everyday life.

States of Mind

Core concept: Wise Mind is the dialectical balance between emotion and reason.

We experience three primary states of mind: emotion mind, reason mind, and Wise Mind.

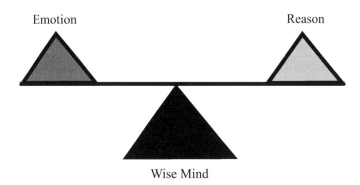

These states of mind exist on a continuum, with Wise Mind being a balance of emotion and reason. Remember that each state of mind is not "good" or "bad"; these judgments are relative and depend on the context of the situation. Instead, seeing what "works" in a given situation is more useful.

Remember that in dialectics, an extreme contains the seed of the opposite. When we are too far in emotion mind, the need for reason arises and vice versa. We are most effective, most of the time, in Wise Mind.

In a Wise Mind place, we validate our emotional experience *and* integrate our ability to use reason. As described in the introduction to Mindfulness, we use our hearts and our heads, being fully present in the moment. In Wise Mind we can reflect without judgment, live our true intentions in spite of how we feel, and *be* in our experiences without being consumed by them.

Wise Mind is grounded in our values (see FAST) and meets the reality of situations effectively. In Wise Mind, we can overcome our conditioned reactions and be responsive instead. *We all have a wise mind!*

The Path to Wise Mind (WM)

Core concept: The What and How skills lead us to Wise Mind.

Wise Mind is less elusive when we understand the skills used to lead us there: Observe, Describe, and Participate are the What skills. In other words, these three skills are *what* we do to get to Wise Mind. Nonjudgmental Stance, One-mindfulness, and Effectiveness are the How skills. In other words, these three skills are *How* we apply the What skills to get to Wise Mind.

Although each What and How skill is described individually, remember that they work together to refine our connection with experience and bring us to Wise Mind. To orient yourself to use these skills, practice the directives of this mantra:

Pause, breath, center ... enter

WHAT SKILLS

Observe: Notice your experience without adding to it or subtracting from it, without amplifying it or pushing it away. Let the experience pass through like clouds drifting in the sky or scenery passing by a car window. Cling to nothing.

Use your senses to gather information. What is seen, heard, smelled, tasted, and touched? What is happening in your mind and body?

Note your feelings, thoughts, behaviors, others, situations, and the environment—look inside *and* outside yourself. Notice what is happening physically in your body and the associated sensations. Direct your attention and decide what enters and what stays out; open and close your mental windows with intention.

Describe: Outline the details of your observations with specific descriptions. Use words to bring your observations to life. Language frequently helps to make sense of experience. Clarify your experience for yourself and others.

Do not get caught in analyzing your thoughts, feelings, sensations, impulses, and urges. Instead, remember that thoughts are just thoughts, feelings are just feelings, sensations are just sensations, and impulses and urges are just impulses and urges. You are not your mind, and these experiences are not commands.

Participate: Observe and Describe bring awareness to experience. Use this awareness to make choices and to become one with your experience. Go from simply watching your experience to being in relation with your experience. Ultimately, *be in* your experience.

Choose whether you want to stay with and relate further to your experience or redirect your Observe and Describe skills. Recognize if you are participating in symptoms or problems and choose to participate in skills instead. Redirect your attention based on your wisdom of what works and not simply out of aversion to your experience or a desire to escape from your experience.

Practice these skills until they are part of you and you can use them flowing from Wise Mind.

HOW SKILLS

Nonjudgmental Stance: Stick to the facts without coloring them with opinions. Focus on who, what, where, when, and how like an objective reporter. Use respectful language to describe yourself, others, and situations. Be impeccable with your words.

Remember that "good" and "bad" judgments are relative and may not be helpful. Sometimes what appears to be desirable can be suffering in disguise, and sometimes problems are hidden opportunities.

Stay away from judgments that amplify or reduce experience or get you stuck in a painful experience by adding suffering. Instead, simply accept what is. (See Radical Acceptance and Everyday Acceptance)

When you observe judgments, gently let go of them. We all judge, so do not amplify your judgments by giving them unneeded power.

One-mindfulness: Focus on one thing with your complete attention. Distractions from inside and outside of you will happen. Practice stepping out of distractions and avoid being consumed by them. Instead, gently notice and let go of distractions that keep you from your focus.

Treat yourself with kindness and compassion as you practice being one-mindful and accept distractions instead of judging them. Do not trade the present moment for judgment mind.

If your attention gets divided, stop and focus your attention on what you choose to experience. Be in the here and now.

Effectiveness: Do what works best based on the demands of the situation and not what you would prefer it to be. Do not spend your energies fighting reality. (See Radical Acceptance and Everyday Acceptance)

Do not act out of judgments and a need to be "right." Instead, stay connected to your goals, priorities, and values and use them as guides to act as skillfully as possible.

Use Willingness to get from point "A" to point "B" to accomplish your goals. Remove your own complications and barriers to get out of your own way.

Train yourself to be responsive to experience rather than reactive to experience.

Focus on Nonjudgmental Stance (NJS)

Core concept: Understand when to use judgments and when to let them go.

Judgments (nonjudgmentally speaking!) are not "good" or "bad" or "right" or "wrong." In fact, judgments can be quite helpful at times when we need to label, categorize, and move on or when we simply want to communicate quickly.

It is easier to say that the weather is "bad" than observing and describing every detail of the forecast to justify staying home during a storm. Similarly, we might say it is a "good" day to quickly let others know that problems have been minimal or handled effectively.

Judgments have likely been useful in other ways too. If most men (or women) have hurt you in life, judgments about that gender might keep you safe psychologically or even physically in some situations.

Judgments are less effective when they become over-generalized or rigid or when we are unable to shift them based on new or different information and experiences. Reliable indications that judgments no longer work include a strong, ongoing negative emotional association and/or chronically failing to meet your wants and needs because of a judgmental mindset. If judgments result in you clashing with a variety of people over time, that might also be a sign that Nonjudgmental Stance could be worthwhile.

To see if judgments might be more or less useful, try to see if they are "Teflon®" judgments or "sticky" judgments. We have no personal investment in or strong emotional reactions to Teflon® judgments. These types of judgments can be readily revised when we take in more or different information. In fact, these judgments can be helpful when we need to quickly make a decision and move on.

Sticky judgments act like tinted or colored glasses that shade almost everything around us. Because we are committed to these judgments, we refuse to take off those glasses to see ourselves, others, situations, and the world in a different light. Sticky judgments do not help us move on but weigh us down like rocks in a backpack. If you find that your "backpack" is full of heavy judgments, it may be time to take it off, put it down, and gently start to remove those rocks (and use one to smash your tinted glasses, metaphorically speaking of course!).

32

Focus on One-mindfulness (OM)

Core concept: We observe divided attention and mindlessness to direct ourselves back to one-mindfulness.

We can clarify One-mindfulness through examples of divided attention and mindlessness. When we find ourselves in these situations, we go back to the What and How skills to be one-mindful.

Continual Partial Attention: Many of us go through our days attending to multiple stimuli simultaneously without giving any one thing our full and complete attention. We eat while watching TV and check our email while in the presence of our families. We think about our problems in the middle of a conversation or during an otherwise positive experience. We talk on the phone while driving and choose to distract from everyday tasks rather than attending to them. We escape the small moments rather than recognizing that life *is* the small moments.

The result is incomplete and disconnected attention and connection. When you notice this continual partial attention, stop, make a choice, and focus on one thing.

Multitasking: We have been misled to believe that multitasking is a strength and is desired. In reality, we can only multitask when behaviors are over-learned or automatic. In these cases, we do not use our conscious minds but instead act like robots.

When we try to multitask with behaviors and in situations that require our conscious attention, we are not actually doing more than one activity at once; we are shifting our attention back and forth. This approach requires much more mental energy and sets us up to make mistakes.

To illustrate, try this multitasking experiment with two independently easy tasks and notice the outcome: First, count from 1 to 26 as quickly as possible, noting the time. Next, say the ABCs as quickly as possible, again noting the time. Add up the times of these two tasks done one-mindfully. Now, try a true multitasking activity. Time yourself as you alternate performing the tasks of counting and reciting the ABCs (e.g., 1 A 2 B 3 C 4 D and so on). Notice the difference in time, energy, and accuracy.

As another example, you may notice that your computer progressively slows as you have more and more functions open. Your computer is programmed to "multitask," but at some point it spends more time switching and reorienting than actually working. It may even shut down. Your computer's limitations mirror our own limited capacity to spread out our focus. Work on doing one thing at a time as a habit.

Automatic Behaviors: Automatic behaviors include anything you can do unconsciously or without thought. While not recommended, most of us can drive, carry on basic conversations, and do most activities of daily living with virtually no attention or connection.

Automatic behaviors can be useful at times. In fact, sometimes automatic behaviors can be highly effective, like when someone automatically follows an over-learned protocol in an emergency situation or when you swerve or hit your brakes to avoid an automobile accident.

The other side of the dialectic is that automatic behaviors remove us from the here and now of life and deprive us of basic pleasures. A great exercise is being mindful of your automatic behaviors step by step with intention. Examples include mindfully preparing and eating meals, driving with your full attention, and taking a shower or bath with awareness of the experience. Any thought or behavior in your day can be attended to one-mindfully.

Sticky Judgments Application

Core concept: Use this exercise to let go of sticky judgments.

Describe one sticky judgment about yourself, others, or situations:

Describe how that sticky judgment needlessly upsets you, weighs you down, or holds you back:

Describe how your life will be different without that sticky judgment:

Commit yourself to slowly (or radically!) get unstuck from that judgment.

Mindfulness Practice and Application

Core concept: These exercises help us practice the skills that lead to Wise Mind.

Try these Mindfulness exercises and create your own. Mindfulness needs to be part of your daily routine. Enjoy!

Attention to Small Moments: Small moments in our lives include those that we do not typically notice or those we take for granted. It may be having a cup of coffee or a cool glass of water, spending a moment with a child or pet, or performing any "normal" activity that goes by without our attention. Enjoyment, peace, and serenity in life happen in the small moments. Each hour, orient yourself to the small moments that you might otherwise miss.

Focus on Senses: Take time to notice what comes through your five senses: what you see, hear, smell, taste, and/or touch. Your senses are your gateway to the world. (See SELF-SOOTHE)

Breathing: We all breathe, and we can all breathe more effectively. Our breath is our anchor and is an excellent way to center ourselves. Take time to breathe mindfully in and out. Stay focused on the sensation of the air coming into your air passages and lungs, holding it, and then letting it out. Use a mantra, such as "in" as you breathe in and "out" as you breathe out, or count each breath from 1 to 10, starting over when you reach 10 or if you lose count.

Another way to breath mindfully is to notice the beginning, middle, and end of each inhalation and exhalation (like how you can hear the beginning, middle, and end of sounds—another mindfulness exercise). Concentrate on the life of each breath going in and out.

Quiet/Still Time: Set time aside each day to be quiet and to experience that quiet. Be one-mindful with the stillness, finding your center and noticing comfort in the moment.

Your Favorite Song (or Album): Listen to your favorite song or album with your full attention. Listen closely to the lyrics and their meaning. Be mindful of each word and phrase. Listen to the sounds of the different instruments. Pay attention to the guitar, bass, drums, vocals, or any other instrument that is central to the music. Notice the production values: Is the song basic or elaborate? Bare bones or highly orchestrated? Be mindful of things you have never noticed in music you have listened to many times.

Your Favorite Show: Watch your favorite TV show, paying attention to the small details. Notice what the actors are wearing, how the sets are designed and decorated, and other elaborate details that go into your show.

The Room You Know So Well: Observe and Describe details that you never noticed about your bedroom, living room, office, or any other place in which you have spent significant time.

10 Details: Anyplace, anywhere, pause and Observe and Describe 10 details you would not have otherwise noticed.

Turn Down the Noise (Or Embrace It):   Turn off all extra sources of noise in your home. If you are not mindfully listening to the radio or TV, turn it off. Work on being present without the competition for your attention. If you are unable to turn down certain noises, practice being mindfully aware of them, noticing them without judgment.

People (Or Anything) Watching: Be a watcher of people, or of anything that might hold your interest. Remember not to judge what you see, but simply let it into and out of your experience like clouds floating through the sky.

One Chore/One Task: Do one chore or one task, such as washing the dishes or folding laundry, with all of your attention and care. Be one-mindful with the experience without adding or subtracting.

"Holding" a Feeling: Hold your present feeling like it is a baby. Calming a distraught baby involves compassion and one-mindfulness. Babies can tell when we are either frustrated or do not want to be with them in the moment. Our feelings are like babies: They can tell when we either reject them or are not fully present with them. Holding your feeling and being mindful of it will usually cause it to diminish in intensity. If not, consider distraction skills.

Interconnection: Contemplate how you are connected to all of the items around you, to your surroundings, to all of the people in your life, and/or to the universe in general.

Relative Thinking: Contemplate the upsides and downsides of any judgment without sticking to any conclusions. See how "good" and "bad" depend on the circumstances and are not fixed.

5/60:   Plan 5 minutes out of every hour to engage in a mindfulness activity. This may include breathing, doing a scan of your body for tension and then relaxing, or one-mindfully accomplishing any task.

Find Your Center: Before engaging in thoughts and behavior, spend a moment to breathe and find your center. Know that finding your center helps you to access your Wise Mind. Practice the directives of the mantra: pause, breath, center ... enter.

Fly Away/Balloon Release: Write whatever you would like to let go of on a helium balloon with a permanent marker. Release the balloon into the sky and watch it with your full attention until it is completely out of your vision. Alternatively, write what you would like to let go of on paper and shred or burn it or place the paper under water and watch the ink wash away and disappear.

Distress Tolerance

Core concept: Distress tolerance helps us cope without making it worse.

We sometimes cope with intense emotions in ways that make our situation worse or neglect our long-term priorities, goals, and values. This coping may work in the short term, but it sabotages our long-term Life Vision. Distress Tolerance skills help us cope in the short term without making our situation worse, and they keep us true to our priorities, goals, values, and Life Vision.

One key to distress tolerance skills is making sure that we consistently practice them when we are not in distress. Practice is how we gain competency with skills. Without practice, trying to use skills in a crisis would be like trying to hit a home run in a big ballgame when you have never picked up a bat.

Another key to distress tolerance is putting a proactive plan together. We often end up reacting to life situations rather than having a plan for how to respond to them. It is difficult to be effective when we react rather than respond.

Luckily, we can simply look to our past to make plans for our future. Our histories have information on what is difficult for us, as well as reactions that have been ineffective versus responses that have worked. We can identify those vulnerabilities and triggering situations and create a plan with new ways to deal with them effectively. Note that your distress tolerance plan will include skills from the other modules too. Remember, you have to combine skills from all modules to be effective.

When you have an effective distress tolerance plan, you can more easily strike the dialectic balance between mindfulness of emotions (especially painful ones) and effective distraction. Finding that balance leads to coping behaviors that are healthy without invalidating your emotions.

Guidelines for Use

Core concept: Understand when and how to use distress tolerance to increase effectiveness.

Distress Tolerance skills are more effective when the guidelines listed here are followed. Like other skills, the effectiveness of distress tolerance is based on knowing when to use these skills and recognizing their limitations.

Distress tolerance is used when we cannot solve a problem. If we *can* solve a problem and it is an okay time to do so, then that will usually be the best strategy.

Sometimes we have the solution to our problem, but it is not a good time to solve it. In that case, we can use distress tolerance until we can solve the problem at a better time.

At other times, we need to use distress tolerance to soothe our emotions before we can solve a problem effectively. In other words, sometimes we know the solution and it is an okay time to proceed, except we are not in Wise Mind enough to be effective. In these cases, we might benefit from distress tolerance before problem-solving.

Ask yourself the following three questions to help you to decide between solving a problem versus using distress tolerance:

1. Am I able to solve the problem? Yes or No. If No, use distress tolerance.
2. Is it an okay time to solve the problem? Yes or No. If No, use distress tolerance.
3. Am I in Wise Mind enough to solve the problem? Yes or No. If No, use distress tolerance.

If you answer Yes to all three questions, then attend to your problem. (See SOLVED)

If you answer Yes to these three questions but avoid attending to and solving your problems, you will eventually end up overwhelmed. We want to avoid the use of distress tolerance to distract from life. The use of excessive distraction keeps piling up our problems.

When we cannot attend to or solve our problems, Distress Tolerance skills replace unhealthy coping behaviors such as self-injury, drinking and drug use, and other behaviors that can damage self-respect or cause other short- and long-term problems.

We can be reluctant to give up our unhealthy coping behaviors even when we know they are destructive to ourselves or others. If you are unsure about giving up a behavior, you may start by simply increasing your options through learning and practicing Distress Tolerance skills. Over time, you may have the confidence to let go of your old ways of just surviving.

As you learn and practice these skills, remember that they are meant to be used in the short term. We need to have many Distress Tolerance skills ready to use for when a crisis lasts for a long time. Keep adding more of these skills to your "toolbox." The more we explore and practice the skills in this module, the more we can manage ourselves and our lives—maybe even proactively changing our vulnerabilities and emotions.

Remember to use your Mindfulness skills along with Distress Tolerance skills. Distress Tolerance skills are much less effective if we continue to focus mentally on our crisis. Mindfulness of the skills we use builds the foundation for successful skill use.

As you start to use Distress Tolerance skills, it is helpful to consider the following dialectics: Attend to the problem versus distract from the problem, and be mindful of the emotion versus be mindful of the distraction. The key to navigating these dialectics is considering the most effective choice in the moment. (See MIDDLE Cs)

My Distress Tolerance Crisis and Safety Plan

Core concept: Develop a plan to manage crisis and safety issues.

Begin to fill out this plan and continue to add to it as you learn more skills. Treat this plan as a "living" document: It needs to be continuously reviewed, practiced, and updated.

Make several copies and always know where to find your plan. It is hard to know what to do when you are in the heat of the moment. That is why you have a written plan.

Give copies to the people in your support system and discuss your use of the plan proactively. Again, practice, practice, practice—practice makes you prepared to be effective in life.

My Reasons for Managing Crisis Effectively and/or Staying Safe: List all of your priorities, goals, values, and people that matter to you. These are your "whys:"

My Strengths and Resources: List what you have going for you. Ask for help if you are unsure:

Warning Signs: These are the signals that you may be in crisis or unsafe or about to be in crisis or unsafe. Be as specific as possible. Look to your history for clues:

Feelings: Ask yourself what you are/were feeling before or during this time:

Thoughts: Ask yourself what you are/were thinking before or during this time:

Behaviors: Ask yourself what you are/were doing and/or not doing before or during this time:

Sensations: Ask yourself what you are/were experiencing physically or in your body before or during this time:

Environment: Ask yourself what your environment is/was like and/or what is/was happening in your environment before or during this time:

Key Triggers: Ask yourself what sets off a crisis and/or being unsafe for you:

Barriers to Skill Use: List what will get in the way of using your skills and this plan *and* list the skills you will use to address each barrier:

Burn the Bridges: Write how you will remove the means to act on urges and be specific:

Self-Care Skills to Use: List all of the ways you can care for yourself during this time:

Distress Tolerance Skills to Use: List specific behaviors:

My Personal Support System: List names and numbers of people/resources you can call, when they are accessible, and the specific interpersonal and other skills you will need to use these supports:

My Professional Support System: List names and numbers of people/resources you can call, when they are accessible, and the specific interpersonal and other skills you will need to use these supports:

My Medications and Dosages:

My Hospital of Choice:

My Commitment: I commit to practicing my plan proactively and during times of crisis. I further commit to be safe and call 911 or go to the hospital BEFORE acting on suicidal urges.

Signed by Client: _____ Date: _____
Original to client; copy to chart

Distract with ACCEPTS

Core concept: Accept distress to effectively work on distraction skills.

When we experience distress or crisis or feel unsafe, we have a few choices. We can work on problem-solving (see SOLVED), be mindful of our painful emotions (see Mindfulness), or work on distraction skills.

Use the acronym *ACCEPTS* to remember the building blocks (**A**ctivities, **C**ontributing, **C**omparisons, **E**motions, **P**ush Away, **T**houghts, **S**ensations) of this skill. These building blocks are described in further detail in the paragraphs that follow.

Activities: Activities help you to decrease depression, anxiety, and other symptoms and can create positive emotions. See the Activities List along with the ROUTINE skill. You need to plan activities as part of your daily routine and follow through with the plans.

Activities work best when they engage you physically and/or mentally. Remember Mindfulness skills (and the other Distress Tolerance skills, too) need to be used in connection to activities.

You may have difficulty with activities because you lack interest or energy. When writers have writer's block, they continue to write anyway, because inspiration finds us when we are at work. If we wait to be interested, we might wait a long time.

You can control the choice to engage in activities, and in time, interest and enjoyment will follow if you do not obsess on it. In other words, mindfully engage in activities without concern for or being caught up in interest or enjoyment. Start with activities that have been interesting and enjoyable in the past.

Use Opposite to Emotion when energy is low and/or DEAR MAN to get others to help you get kick-started. The first law of physics applies: A body at rest tends to stay at rest, and a body in motion tends to stay in motion.

Describe how you can use **Activities**:

Contributing: Contributing helps you get out of yourself and your distress and into participating with others and in the world. We all need a break from ourselves sometimes. Contributing also helps you feel connected and less alone, and it creates positive feelings.

Contribute in small but impactful ways: Smile at others, give compliments, hold a door, or do a favor. Thoughtful and unexpected acts of kindness, random or not, fit the bill. Let someone else have a parking spot or move ahead of you in line. Help out others, be part of a team effort, and participate. Simply listening to others can be a great contribution, too. Also consider longer-term ways of contributing, such as volunteering.

Describe how you can use **Contributing**:

Comparisons: Comparisons bring perspective to your current situation. You can compare yourself to other times when you have dealt with more difficult problems or been less effective with skills. You can also compare yourself to others who struggle with even greater problems than you. We want to remember to validate ourselves as we use comparisons—we can experience tough times *and* have perspective through this skill.

Describe how you can use **Comparisons:**

Emotions: Seek out activities, events, and thoughts that create feelings that are different than the painful ones you are experiencing. (See Opposite to Emotion and Build Positive Experience) Remember that emotions can be influenced by what you choose to do and what you choose to think about.

Listen to music that creates different emotions: loud and fast music when fatigued, calming music when anxious or upset, or uplifting music when sad. Watch favorite shows or movies, fondly remember fun times (without comparing them to your current situation), or work on a project. (See Build Mastery)

Alternatively, sometimes we can use emotions to validate our feelings. For example, we can listen to melancholy music when sad. However, be careful not to get stuck! The concept is self-validation, not wallowing.

Describe how you can use **Emotions:**

Push Away: Put away distress by mentally locking it in a box and putting it on a shelf in a locked room. Make the imagery as vivid as possible, practicing it over and over. Say "This is a tomorrow problem" and then focus on something else. Or, write something about the problem down and put it away in a drawer or someplace where you will remember to find it when you are ready.

Remember to take out your distress or problem at a safe time in the future to attend to it. Putting and pushing away is a short-term strategy.

Describe how you can use **Push Away:**

Thoughts: Mindfully focus on distracting thoughts. (See One-mindfulness) You can only think about one thing at a time, and your distress may diminish when you think about something else. The classic example is counting to 100 when angry; thinking about something else (counting) helps us to cool down and be more rational.

Read a magazine or book, do Sudoku or other puzzles, or think about inspirational sayings and quotes. Bring your thoughts mindfully to other Distress Tolerance skills or activities.

Describe how you can use **Thoughts:**

Sensations: Sensations include anything that is physically vigorous or actively awakens your senses. The skill is different from the Self-Sooth skills in that it seeks to stimulate rather than relax.

Take a brisk walk or engage in exercise, such as running or weight-lifting. Get into a hot or cold bath or shower or splash cold water on your face. Engage your senses with loud music, bold colors, or strong tastes or smells.

Some people hold ice cubes or a frozen orange when in distress as a substitute for self-injury because the physical pain distracts from the emotional pain. These practices can work in a "harm-reduction" approach, meaning they can be used as safer step-down techniques when you are trying to stop self-injury but are not completely ready yet. Remember that ultimately we want to learn that you do not need physical pain to cope with emotional pain.

Describe how you can use **S̲ensations**:

Self-soothe (SS)

Core concept: Create relaxation with a mindful connection to the senses.

Self-soothe involves entering into the world around us through our five main senses individually or in a multisensory way. We can also soothe ourselves mentally and spiritually. Remember that Self-Soothe requires the use of Mindfulness skills.

Sight: Notice what is around you and see the details. Look at pictures or take your own photos. Look at art or do your own drawing or another artistic pursuit that involves vision.

See people, pets, and your favorite possessions and be mindful of what is attractive or visually pleasing. Alternatively, see the beauty in "ordinary" objects or your everyday surroundings.

Look at nature and the landscape around you. See trees and leaves sway in the wind. Look at the sky, the sun, the moon, and the stars. Watch a candle or fire.

Describe how you can Self-soothe with **Sight:**

Sound: Listen to sounds that comfort or notice complete silence. Concentrate on pleasant music, white noise, or the sound of a washing machine or dishwasher if those sounds please you. When listening to music, isolate and focus on each instrument or voice with intention.

Close your eyes, be still, and hear what is happening in your environment. Listen for novel sounds or for sonic patterns and rhythms you never noticed.

Describe how you can Self-soothe with **Sound:**

Smell: Put on a favorite cologne or perfume and breathe it in. Smell clean and fresh laundry or sheets. Use incense or other scented products you enjoy. Close your eyes and inhale, choosing to linger on the smell.

Deeply inhale the smells of cooking or baking and your food before eating it or without eating it. Like with sound, noticing the absence of smells can be soothing for some people.

Describe how you can Self-soothe with **Smell:**

Taste: Enjoy each small bite of food or sip of a drink mindfully. Eat one piece of candy or have a small treat with your full attention. Pretend it will be the last time you will eat something and savor each morsel.

DO NOT mindlessly eat to comfort yourself or eat excessively to self-soothe; these approaches are not skillful.

Describe how you can Self-soothe with **Taste:**

Touch: Touch and pet a dog or cat or other animal. Use DEAR MAN to ask for a hug or massage from someone or rub and stroke your own neck or body. Put oils or lotions on your skin.

Wear comfortable clothing or get under a warm, soft blanket or clean, cool sheets. Mindfully notice what your body is in connection with and seek out what pleases.

Describe how you can Self-soothe with **Touch:**

Multisensory: Integrate your senses into a rich experience. Make a meal special with nice dishes, place settings, candles, and relaxing music. Spend time outside, focusing on each sense, deciding what sense to attend to in the context of the total experience. Go to a movie with intricate sound and visuals while also noticing the smells of popcorn and the comfort of the seat.

While we can experience each sense individually, the idea here is to create a holistic sensory experience where you chose to attend to each element in connection to the whole. Notice how each sense can compliment the others in a total experience.

Describe how you can Self-soothe by **Combining Senses**:

Mind Sense: Engage in those parts of your mental life that bring you relaxation and happiness. Examples include peaceful thoughts, affirmations, and meditations as well as daydreams and fantasies.

Describe how you can Self-soothe through your **Mind Sense**:

Spiritual Sense: Your spiritual sense is an individually defined sense of connection to a higher power, spirit, or nature. This sense, less tangible than the others, can create peace, serenity, and well-being.

We Self-soothe with a spiritual sense through mindful reflections, rituals, and contemplation.

Describe how you can Self-soothe through your **Spiritual Sense:**

SELF-SOOTHE APPLICATION

Core concept: Use this exercise to overcome barriers to the practice of Self-soothe.

For most of us, the concept of Self-soothe is straightforward, but allowing ourselves to engage in these skills or addressing other barriers may be more difficult. Use this worksheet to identify Self-soothe skills and other skills to overcome barriers.

Describe how you can use Self-soothe skills:

Describe barriers to Self-soothe skills (e.g., judgments about self, judgments about deserving, environmental, etc.):

Describe other skills you will use to address each barrier:

Describe how your life will be different when you practice Self-soothe:

Urge Surfing (US)

Core concept: Accept painful emotions and urges and ride the ebbs and flows.

Urge Surfing involves accepting feelings and urges rather than pushing away, fighting, or amplifying them. This approach requires Mindfulness and being nonjudgmental. We are watching and being with the experience without trying to influence or change it. In some ways, this is the opposite of our natural tendency to escape or fix an uncomfortable state. Paradoxically, urge surfing gives us control over what feels uncontrollable.

A surfer goes with the flow and rides a wave to its natural conclusion. High feelings and urges seem like they will not end when we are in the thick of them, often leading us to judge and amplify the experience and/or to act impulsively. Instead, we want to ride them until they ebb and wash out.

You probably have "surfed" urges in life without realizing it. Think about a time you had a strong craving without acting on it or otherwise changing it. The peak of those moments can be hard, but chances are the urge ultimately faded out without you doing anything about it.

To urge surf, we simply Observe the natural ups and downs of emotions and urges. Start by checking in and noting the intensity level from 1 to 10 or simply note whether it is low, medium, or high.

As you continue to Observe, periodically recheck the intensity. You can even chart the intensity level every 5 minutes to get a more objective picture of the ups and downs in actual time (this is a nice way to assess the accuracy of our perceptions of "psychological time"; situations tend to seem longer when we are in distress).

As you practice this skill, you may need to mix in some other Distress Tolerance skills if you get too overwhelmed. Remember to focus on what works. Even world-class surfers stay off of the waves if they are too intense and unsafe!

Bridge Burning (BB)

Core concept: Remove the means of acting on harmful urges.

Burning the bridge typically has a negative connotation. That is, we have been told throughout life *not* to burn our bridges.

Bridge Burning in DBT has a different meaning. It means that we actively seek to remove the means or the "bridge" between a harmful urge and our ability to act on it. The following examples of this skill help illustrate the point.

BRIDGE BURNING WITH ALCOHOL AND/OR DRUGS:

- Remove all alcohol and drugs from your home
- Remove all alcohol- and drug-related objects and paraphernalia from your home (e.g., cocktail glasses, wine opener, pipes, lighters, and/or anything associated with use)
- Erase the numbers of using friends, associates, and dealers from your phone
- Stay away from bars, liquor stores, and locations associated with use, changing your routines and routes to actively avoid them
- Mix up and change rituals associated with use
- Think of other ways to avoid using

BRIDGE BURNING WITH SELF-INJURY AND/OR SUICIDAL URGES:

- Remove razors, lighters, and other self-injury tools
- Mix up and change rituals associated with self-injury
- Remove the specific method of acting on suicide
- Tell others when you are unsafe and need help
- Go to the hospital <u>before</u> acting on suicidal urges
- Think of other methods for preventing self-injury

BRIDGE BURNING WITH SPENDING:

- Cut up credit cards (if you need to keep one, freeze it in water so it will take longer to access it)
- Have someone else (trustworthy) keep extra money when urges are high
- Stay away from stores, the mall, online shopping, and/or TV shopping
- Think of other ways to avoid spending

BRIDGE BURNING WITH HOPELESS RELATIONSHIPS:

- Erase the other person's number from your phone
- Block the other person's number
- Route emails from the other person to your "junk mail folder"
- Fill your free time with activities and healthy people
- Think of other methods for avoiding hopeless relationships

Bridge Burning works best in conjunction with other skills. When we remove the ability to act on harmful behaviors, we need to replace them with something new and skillful.

BRIDGE BURNING (BB) APPLICATION

Core concept: Use this exercise to remove the means to act on your harmful behavior.

Describe how you can use the Bridge Burning skill with a harmful behavior (e.g., self-injury, drinking or drug use, spending, promiscuous sex, overeating). Be specific about how the means to act will be removed:

Describe the new behaviors and skills you will use to replace the old behavior:

Describe how you and others will benefit from effective Bridge Burning (e.g., how you and others will feel, how it will affect your self-respect, what other practical benefits will occur):

Describe how your life will be different when you burn bridges to your harmful behavior(s):

Describe how you will acknowledge and celebrate your effective Bridge Burning:

IMPROVE the Moment

Core concept: Make the here and now better when in distress.

Like ACCEPTS, these skills provide healthy distractions.

Use the acronym *IMPROVE* to remember the building blocks (**I**magery, **M**eaning, **P**rayer, **R**elaxation, **O**ne thing or step at a time, **V**acation, **E**ncouragement) of this skill. These building blocks are described in further detail in the paragraphs that follow.

Imagery: Your mind is powerful. (Think of times when you have distressed yourself with negative imagery.) You can harness the power of positive imagery to feel better and more relaxed. Concentrate on a scene in your mind (a beach, the forest, a safe and happy place). Your mind can convince your body that it is there.

Use guided imagery with a CD. Practice skill use in your mind's eye (proven effective in sports). Enter a daydream. Consider practicing imagery before bedtime as part of your sleep routine.

As distractions creep in, gently let them go and refocus.

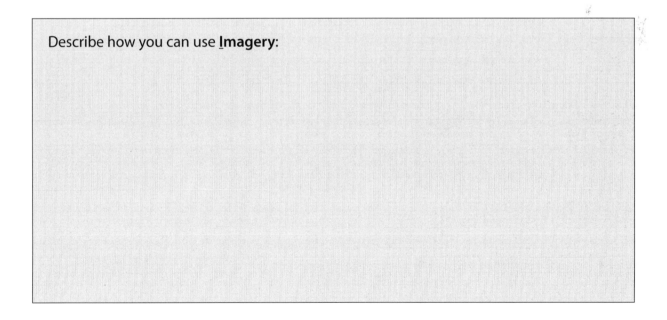

Describe how you can use **Imagery:**

Meaning: Validate that the cloud is there *and* find the silver lining. Is there an opportunity in this problem? What is the lesson or the learning that will come from your difficulties? Victor Frankl, renowned existential psychiatrist and concentration camp survivor, once said, "If you can find a why, you can tolerate almost any how."

Describe how you can use **Meaning:**

Prayer: Pray for strength and resolve in distressful times. Seek connection with and guidance from your higher power. Avoid "why me" or bargaining prayers; those prayers tend to demoralize us rather than build us up.

As an alternative, "talk" to anyone important to you: A deceased relative you loved, a person you admire (whether you know him/her or not), or anyone who helps you feel connected outside yourself.

Describe how you can use **Prayer:**

Relaxation: Practice breathing exercises (see Mindfulness), Self-soothe skills, progressive muscle relaxation with each major muscle group, or anything that calms you.

Describe how you can use **Relaxation:**

One Thing or Step at a Time: When overwhelmed, go back to the most important priority again and again. If you have many problems, pick the most important one to focus on or the one you have the most resources to solve. In the context of solving problems, taking one step at a time helps to manage your distress.

Describe how you can use **One Thing or Step at a Time:**

Vacation: Most of us cannot take a real vacation when in distress or maybe even at all. Vacation means taking a break when we are in distress (or before we are in distress). Step outside, breath fresh air, and take a short walk. Spend 10 minutes listening to music or surfing the Internet. Talk with a friend or coworker. "Take a load off." Plan some time for yourself as a part of your routine.

Remember to keep these "vacations" brief. We want to take a break from problems but not let them continue to build.

Describe how you can use **Vacation:**

Encouragement: We all talk to ourselves, so we might as well say something positive! Validate your feelings and then encourage yourself like you would a close friend. Life is not impossible; it just feels that way sometimes.

Describe how you can use **Encouragement:**

Pros and Cons (P&C)

Core concept: Pros and Cons lead us to Wise Mind decisions.

We can use Pros and Cons any time that we struggle with a decision. This skill helps us weigh the options in light of expected results in both the short and the long term. This skill is proactive and leads us to Wise Mind before committing to any action.

If we use Pros and Cons to decide whether we want to engage in a harmful behavior, often we will find that the urge has subsided by the time the exercise is complete. To use this skill, start by identifying your basic choices. Examples include drinking or using drugs versus staying sober, using self-injury versus staying safe, and practicing an old behavior versus practicing a skill.

When you have identified the basic choices, plug them into the worksheet that follows. After you have determined both short- and long-term pros and cons, check to see if you are in Wise Mind and make a decision. If you find that you are not in Wise Mind, table your decision and try another skill.

Pros and Cons (P&C) Application Example

My Basic Choices Are: Using self-injury versus using skills

Short-Term PROS of Self-Injury	Short-Term CONS of Self-Injury
Numbed my feelings! Worked Blood grounded me know	Missed chance to use plan Worried about upcoming group Had to hide it

Long-Term PROS of Self-Injury	Long-Term CONS of Self-Injury
None really	Lost trust Lost self-respect More scars Shame sets me up

Versus

Short-Term PROS of Skill Use	Short-Term CONS of Skill Use
No need to lie or cover up Feel good if I make it No hassle with blood and stuff NO CHANGE ANALYSIS!!	Hard and might not work Don't know Maybe more emotional pain

Long-Term PROS of Skill Use	Long-Term CONS of Skill Use
RESPECT! Learn to handle life and get somewhere	More expectations? Pressure, I don't know

My Decision: Skills, I guess!!

Pros and Cons (P&C) Application

My Basic Choices Are_____ versus_____ .

Short-Term PROS of _____	Short-Term CONS of _____

Long-Term PROS of _____	Long-Term CONS of _____

Versus

Short-Term PROS of _____	Short-Term CONS of _____

Long-Term PROS of _____	Long-Term CONS of _____

My Decision: _____

Grounding Yourself (GY)

Core concept: Grounding exercises bring you back to the here and now.

Grounding exercises help us when we drift from the present moment or when we struggle with dissociation or with feeling unreal. Leaving reality is a skill when reality would be too painful for anyone bear. At the same time, leaving reality is less effective when we are distressed but not in imminent psychological and/or physical danger.

Practice these exercises proactively, and they will decrease symptoms of dissociation and derealization. Remember to bring your Mindfulness skills along:

- Open your eyes and Observe and Describe your surroundings in detail.
- Who or what is around you? You are here, now. The more detail, no matter how minor, the better.
- Work your senses: Name what you see, hear, smell, and touch right here and now, again using as many details as possible.
- Use the Sensations skill from ACCEPTS. Practice the different variations of Sensations.
- Observe your body in contact with your chair. Feel your back, behind, and back of your legs in connection with the chair. Feel your arms in connection with the armrests or your lap. Feel your feet firmly planted on the ground. Now think about how your body is connected to the chair, which is connected to the floor, which is connected to the building, which is connected to the earth.
- Breathe slowly and deeply, counting your breaths.
- Get up and stretch out, feeling your body and moving about.
- Repeat a mantra like "this is now and not then."
- Think of other ways to ground yourself.

Radical Acceptance (RA)

Core concept: Acceptance decreases suffering.

At times, we have great pain due to trauma, difficult life circumstances, and losses. Suffering is part of everyone's life.

If we are unable to accept situations that cause pain, the result is being stuck and trapped in chronic suffering. The refusal to have a relationship with our suffering creates unending suffering. Paradoxically, we decrease suffering by being willing to accept it and relate to it rather than fight it. We may still have pain to tolerate, but there will be a qualitative difference in our experience of it.

Acceptance instead of resistance releases our resources to move forward. When we find ourselves in pain, we have four basic choices:

1. Change the Situation Causing Us Pain: This change may involve ending a hopeless relationship or leaving a dead-end job, or it might involve seeking medical advice or trying to solve some other problem. Changing the situation involves a realistic appraisal of what is and what the options are, grounded in values. (See SOLVED) What would you be willing to do to end suffering? (See Willingness)

2. Change How You See or What You Think About the Situation: Can you find the upside, silver lining, or meaning in the pain? (See Meaning) Would more dialectical thoughts help? (See MIDDLE Cs and REASON) Remember that our minds can be powerful in overcoming obstacles, including suffering. Is it a tragedy or "good practice?" Is it a terrible situation or a situation to teach strength, patience, or resilience?

3. Radically Accept the Situation: Give up fighting reality and release your psychological resources to move forward. When you accept, you might still have to tolerate pain but you are no longer adding to it. Radical Acceptance means you are willing to experience a situation or state without trying to change it, protest it, or escape it. You will be in a relationship with the pain.

4. Stay Stuck in Suffering Until You Are Ready to Accept Reality: Radical acceptance springs from deep within ourselves and requires that we turn our minds over and over toward accepting.

Remember that acceptance is *not* approval, liking it, or giving in. When we recognize, acknowledge, and accept a problem or reality, we actually take control of our lives and emotional health.

Acceptance is freedom because it allows us to be effective with what is rather than stuck in denial. Acceptance is the prerequisite to change.

It is helpful to know that Radical Acceptance is a process similar to Kubler-Ross's (2005) stages of acceptance:

1. **Denial:** Not believing our loss, problem, or situation is real.
2. **Anger:** Being angry about why this has or is happening to us.
3. **Bargaining:** Trying to make a deal with someone or a higher power to change reality.
4. **Depression:** Feeling despondent as reality sets in.
5. **Acceptance:** Acknowledging reality without fighting.

These stages do not always happen in sequence. Instead, we often go back and forth in the process, sometimes getting stuck in one stage and/or skipping others. When you experience these stages and emotions, you are in the process of acceptance.

In the words of William James, "Be willing to have it so. Acceptance of what has happened is the first step to overcoming the consequences of any misfortune." Allow it to be so and experience the pain. You are not and do not need to be the story of your suffering.

RADICAL ACCEPTANCE (RA) APPLICATION

Core concept: Use this exercise to practice Radical Acceptance in a painful situation.

Describe a situation that causes suffering:

Describe changes you could make to the situation if possible:

Describe what you can realistically change through problem-solving and/or shifting your thoughts:

Describe what you may need to Radically Accept:

Describe other skills you may need to practice Radical Acceptance of this situation:

Describe how your life will be different when you have Radically Accepted this situation:

Describe how you will acknowledge and celebrate your freedom from suffering:

Everyday Acceptance (EA)

Core concept: Adopting an accepting attitude each day will change your life.

Radical Acceptance is the skill used to deal with painful and difficult-to-accept situations. Practice acceptance in everyday situations to orient yourself to the practice of acceptance. What is meant by Everyday Acceptance? Consider the following examples:

- You have to wait in a long line
- Your spouse, partner, or friend is in a lousy mood
- The delivery person is 30 minutes late
- Your coworker makes a mistake
- A guitar string breaks
- Homework is assigned
- A friend cancels a date
- Dinner is not your favorite
- Your favorite sports team is losing
- You run out of paper towels (or some everyday convenience)
- The weather does not fit your plans
- A task needs to be completed
- Someone cuts you off in traffic
- MTV™ shows only 10 seconds of your favorite video
- You forget to save changes to a computer file
- You step in gum
- A dish breaks
- Your toddler acts like a toddler
- Gas prices have risen
- Your partner forgot to pick up milk

We often cause ourselves to feel frustrated, annoyed, anxious, and stressed out by these common inconveniences. Instead, we can save our resources by meeting these small realities with Everyday Acceptance rather than resistance.

Do not confuse this approach to life as giving in, being walked on, or remaining helpless. Many of these problems have solutions or interventions that are needed (e.g., using assertiveness, running to the store, changing the channel, setting a boundary). However, the use of everyday acceptance allows us to have the emotional balance to solve our everyday problems more effectively. Let it be so, and then deal with it effectively.

Willingness (W)

Core concept: Use willingness versus willfulness when stuck.

Many of us learned that "where there is a will there is a way." In other words, our shortcomings come from a lack of willpower.

This belief system is the opposite of what DBT teaches. Sometimes we need to exert our will, but often Willingness is more effective. Where there is Willingness there is a way.

This approach works because Willingness aligns us with the realities of a situation rather than pitting ourselves against them. Fighting reality (or anything) rarely creates an effective outcome. Think about power struggles and how ineffective they can be for everybody involved.

Meeting others and situations where they are at instead of where we wish they were frees us to be effective. The parallels to Radical Acceptance and Everyday Acceptance are apparent. Willingness also fits with Effectiveness in the Mindfulness Module. Check your priorities, goals, and values to help find your Willingness!

When faced with a problem (and/or stuck in willfulness) ask yourself what you are willing to do to:

- End your suffering
- Solve a problem—yours, someone else's, or a shared one
- Create a satisfying life

With time and practice, you will find that Willingness allows you to be more peaceful and effective in life.

Problem-Solving

Core concept: A systematic approach helps to solve problems.

Problems of different types and levels of difficulty frequent our lives. If we do not actively work to solve our problems, they grow in number and size, and we end up chronically overwhelmed or even paralyzed by them.

Start by being aware of problems and accepting them as they come up. Notice when problems happen and then specifically define them in nonjudgmental language. Next, begin to identify options to solve those problems that cause distress.

Many of us do not have a method for solving problems. We try to solve problems by trial and error or in a haphazard manner. These approaches work sometimes, but tend to be ineffective overall.

Another difficulty comes from emotion mind "problem-solving." We want to validate our feelings and consider the information that comes from them, but staying stuck with emotions leads to emotion-focused coping and mood-congruent behavior. Emotion-focused coping and mood-congruent behavior can work in the short term, but they often cause more problems in the long term.

Instead, it is beneficial to balance our emotions with our reason to reach a Wise Mind place to work through problems and difficulties. In our Wise Mind, we connect with our priorities, goals, and values and can engage in an effective approach to problem-solving.

Using SOLVED (SO)

Core concept: Use this systematic approach to solve problems.

Use the acronym *SOLVED* to remember the building blocks (**S**tep Back and Be Objective, **O**bserve Available Options, **L**imit Barriers, **V**alues Driven, **E**ffectiveness First, **D**ialectical Thought and Action) of this skill. These building blocks are described in further detail in the paragraphs that follow.

<u>S</u>tep Back and Be Objective: Observe and Describe from reason mind or Wise Mind. What is the problem in nonjudgmental terms? Stick to the facts: who, what, where, when, how, and why. Write it down.

<u>O</u>bserve Available Options: Brainstorm and list as many options as you can. Then determine what options are available. Remember to accept the realities of both the problem and the possible solutions. Also list the resources you can use at this step. Use DEAR MAN to ask for ideas, help, and guidance if needed.

<u>L</u>imit Barriers (Emotional and Environmental):   Remove barriers that stand between you and a potential solution. Do not get in your own way. Use Acceptance, Willingness, and Nonjudgmental Stance. Do not amplify or minimize your problems. Gauge the level of your problem and address it in a manner-of-fact way. Identify whether barriers exist in your environment and address them as needed. Again, use DEAR MAN to ask for ideas, help, and guidance if needed.

<u>V</u>alues Driven (What Are Your Priorities and Goals?):   Use your priorities, goals, and values as your compass. (See FAST) Values will not lead you astray in the long term; they will be the foundation of solutions that work. From your available options, pick the solution that best builds your self-respect.

<u>E</u>ffectiveness First: What will work? The most effective solutions will not always be your preferred solutions. (See Effectiveness) Accept that life has problems and solve this one so you can get on to the next one.

Dialectical Thought and Action: Solutions sometimes come with conflict. Conflict is resolved through dialectics. Use MIDDLE Cs with thoughts and actions, and remember that effective, values-driven solutions often come from the middle ground.

Then make a decision and take action. Evaluate the outcomes and use the SOLVED process to readjust your approach and the solution to your problem if needed.

SOLVED (SO) Application

Core concept: Use this worksheet to solve problems.

Step back and describe your problem from Wise Mind:

Describe the options and resources available to you:

Describe your barriers and the skills that you will use to address them:

Describe your priorities, goals, and values and how they can guide your solution:

Use the above information to describe what will work:

Describe your solution and action plan:

Describe how your life will be different when you solve this problem:

Describe how you will acknowledge and celebrate reaching an effective solution:

Emotion Regulation

Core concept: Emotion regulation changes our relationship to feelings.

Emotion Regulation has several purposes. First, we want to identify our feelings and then, more importantly, we want to understand the process by which they happen. When we see how events and interpretations color our emotions, we can positively influence them and get unstuck from negative emotional patterns.

Next, we want to learn how to change our relationship to our feelings. Instead of judging or attempting to "get rid" of negative emotions, we want to accept them and try to understand their message. A curious and understanding approach to our feelings can replace fear and suffering.

As we change our relationship to our feelings, we can learn to "hold" them mindfully. Mindfulness of emotions reduces suffering because we are not adding to emotional pain (although we need to balance this approach with distraction skills).

When we gain a better understanding of our emotions, we can then work on decreasing our emotional vulnerabilities through more effective self-care skills and through scheduling positive experiences. We will also learn how to continue positive feelings through Mood Momentum and get unstuck from negative feelings through Opposite to Emotion.

To begin, we want to understand that emotional health and well-being is a dialectical balance between physical and mental health.

Well-Being

Core dialectic: Well-being involves having a balance between physical and mental health.

Our minds and bodies are connected, and it is difficult to have a general sense of well-being when we do not balance physical and mental health. The PLEASED skills (see next section) teach basic self-care skills to improve and maintain physical health so we can feel better all around.

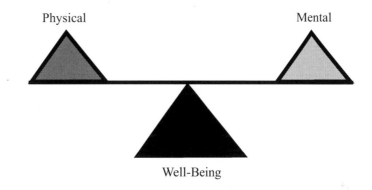

As we learn PLEASED, we want to consider how we can improve our well-being through our goals for both physical and mental health.

Describe your goals for improving **physical** health:

Describe your goals for improving **mental** health:

Describe how your life will be different when you improve your well-being:

Describe how you will acknowledge and celebrate a greater sense of well-being:

Using PLEASED (PL)

Core concept: Self-care skills promote well-being and reduce emotional vulnerability.

Self-care is the foundation of feeling well and being ready to weather emotional storms.

Use the acronym *PLEASED* to remember the building blocks (**P**hysical Health, **L**ist Resources and Barriers, **E**at Balanced Meals, **A**void Drugs and Alcohol, **S**leep between 7 and 10 Hours, **E**xercise 20 to 60 Minutes, **D**aily) of this skill. These building blocks are described in further detail in the paragraphs that follow.

Physical Health: We must attend to our physical health to feel well. That means staying current on our health through regular medical checkups and engaging in proactive skills and behaviors that keep our bodies healthy. It also means treating illness when it arises and complying with medical advice. Take medications as prescribed (or consult your prescriber) and make life changes to minimize use of medications when indicated. Always consider how your physical health may be impacting your mental health.

List Resources and Barriers: Resources include skills we might already use (like O2E, Pros and Cons, and Willingness), people who support us, and having knowledge about health and wellness. Identify strengths and all available resources for each part of the PLEASED skill. Barriers also abound with PLEASED skills. Develop a plan to use skills to address barriers.

Eat Balanced Meals: Eat three balanced meals plus a couple of healthy snacks mindfully throughout the day. Fruits, vegetables, whole grains, and lean protein are must-haves. Eat "whole" (unprocessed or minimally processed) or single-ingredient foods when possible. Drink 10 full glasses of water a day. Avoid eating too much or too little and minimize sugars, saturated fats, and food or beverages with little or no nutritional value. Replace "diets" with lifestyle changes and keep current on reputable nutritional information. Start small and build on success. Consult with a physician or nutritionist if needed.

<u>A</u>void Drugs and Alcohol: The risks associated with drugs and alcohol, along with the emotional, physical, relational, financial, and other effects, can make their use problematic. If you find you need larger amounts to reach a "desired" effect and/or experience an inability to cut down or quit use, you probably need some help and support.

<u>S</u>leep Between 7 and 10 Hours: Sleep is important to regulate our moods. Find an amount of sleep that works for you. See the instructions in the "Sleep Routine" section for more information.

<u>E</u>xercise 20 to 60 Minutes: Exercise for a minimum of 20 minutes three to five times weekly. Balanced exercise will positively impact almost any symptom of mental illness. Find natural ways of exercising, like taking stairs, parking at the far end of a parking lot, and playing with pets or children. Humans are not biologically designed to be sedentary, so movement is vital. Consult a physician with concerns about starting an exercise routine.

<u>D</u>aily: PLEASED skills need to be daily habits for you to reap their great benefits. Record PLEASED skills on a Diary Card (see "Diary Card" section) and/or include them in written routines and schedules.

PLEASED (PL) APPLICATION

Core concept: Use this worksheet to problem-solve and establish PLEASED skills.

Describe your motivation to improve self-care skills (think of priorities, goals, and values):

Describe your strengths and resources to use PLEASED:

Describe your barriers to using PLEASED:

Describe the skills you will use to address your barriers:

Describe your action plan to start today (share your action plan with others and get started!):

Describe how your life will be different when you use effective PLEASED skills:

Describe how you will acknowledge and celebrate your effective use of PLEASED:

Sleep Routine

Core concept: Sleep routines build healthy sleep patterns.

Many times we try to solve sleep difficulties with medication without trying behavioral interventions. The following suggestions will greatly improve sleep for most of us. However, to be effective, these suggestions must be used nightly for a period of weeks and maintained over the long term. Your efforts will reap benefits and will probably be enjoyable, too.

- Create a sleep routine that begins at least 1 hour before going to bed. Like landing an airplane, healthy sleep involves getting into a pattern and getting the landing gear down well ahead of time. A sleep routine should consist of relaxing activities that cue the mind and body for sleep. Deep breathing, muscle relaxation, and mindfulness work well in a sleep routine.
- Establish consistent sleep and wake times. Avoid using the "snooze" button on your alarm clock.
- The bed should be for sleeping and intimacy only. Wakeful activities in bed confuse the mind and body, and the bed no longer becomes a cue for sleep and rest.
- Create a relaxing environment. A clean and uncluttered environment with fresh bed linens and comfortable blankets and pillows will help create the conditions for sleep. Also, block out sources of light and keep the temperature at a comfortable level, preferably a few degrees cooler than during daytime.
- Avoid alcohol, caffeine, and nicotine for 4 hours (or more) before bedtime.
- Avoid heavy meals and spicy foods before bedtime.
- Avoid any stimulation before bedtime, including arguments or conflict, vigorous activity, or anything else that is likely to activate your mind and body.
- Get exercise during the daytime.
- Avoid daytime napping.
- If you are unable to sleep after 20 minutes, get up and do something boring and/or relaxing until you are sleepy and ready to return to bed.

List other ways to create an effective sleep routine:

Build Mastery (BM)

Core concept: Complete tasks to feel competent and in control.

We all have those daily tasks that lead us to feel in control when completed. The flip side is that when these tasks build up, we feel more overwhelmed and out of control.

For example, basic activities of daily living (see ROUTINE) often need our attention. The following brief list includes basic Build Mastery activities for many of us:

- Hygiene (e.g., brushing teeth, cleaning self, wearing clean clothes)
- Doing the dishes
- Shopping for food and necessities
- Cleaning whatever needs it
- Doing laundry
- Accomplishing important tasks or chores
- Opening mail and/or paying bills
- Completing homework or work tasks
- Tending to our children or pets
- Maintaining a certain level of organization

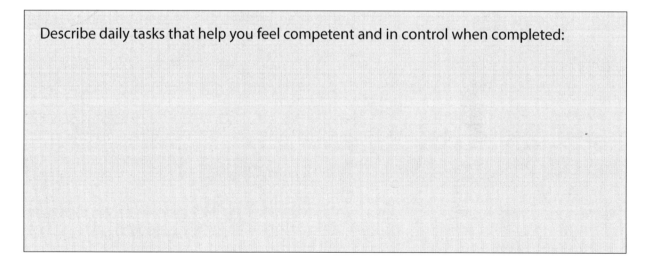

Describe daily tasks that help you feel competent and in control when completed:

Build Mastery skills also include taking on realistic challenges and working toward goals. Here are some examples:

- Practicing virtually any skill
- Developing a hobby
- Exercising
- Taking steps to resolve a problem
- Accomplishing tasks outside your comfort zone
- Dealing with an interpersonal issue
- Standing up for yourself
- Volunteering
- Doing your best in a tough situation

Technically, any attempt to be effective or any accomplishment could be a Build Mastery technique.

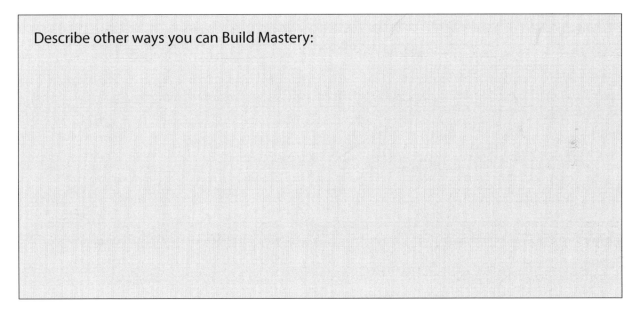

Describe other ways you can Build Mastery:

Be mindful of your efforts and give yourself due credit. We frequently dismiss those things in life that we "should" be doing or are expected to do. We invalidate ourselves by saying those efforts are no big deal and are not worthy of recognition. Alternatively, we minimize their importance or get into judgments about what we did not do as a way to erase our efforts.

As a rule of thumb, if you tend to judge yourself when you think you have not made enough of an effort or have not accomplished something, then you deserve credit for the effort or accomplishment when you do try and when you get something done. Using Build Mastery skills help us feel better, decrease our emotional vulnerability, and increase our self-respect.

Describe how your life will be different when you effectively use Build Mastery:

Describe how you will acknowledge and celebrate your effective use of Build Mastery:

Feelings Model

Core concept: Knowing how feelings happen helps us influence them.

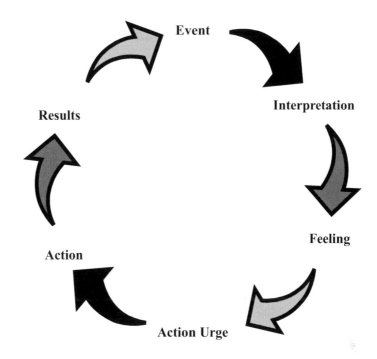

Event: Emotions begin with events, and events can be internal (within us) or external (in our environment). Think of examples of both internal and external events. Use Mindfulness skills to connect an emotion to its source.

Interpretation: How we interpret events has a tremendous influence on what we feel. Use Mindfulness skills to check interpretations (self-talk) of events. Ask if your interpretation works in the situation. Are there other ways of looking at the situation? (Use REASON) Is the interpretation from Wise Mind? Is Nonjudgmental Stance needed?

Feeling: Use Observe and Describe to notice the emotional experience. What is happening in the body (e.g., muscle relaxation or tension, heart rate)? What is happening externally with the body (e.g., facial expressions, posture)? Name the emotion. Remember to observe the experience nonjudgmentally.

Also, try to see if another feeling is underneath what you Observe and Describe on the surface. For example, hurt or embarrassment might underlie anger or guilt, and shame might underlie depression. Getting to the feelings underneath the surface emotion increases understanding. Increased understanding creates more options.

Action Urge/Action: What is the emotion urging or pulling you toward? Or, is an action already happening? Seek clues from your urges and behaviors. Are action urges and actions flowing from Wise Mind? Remember to validate your emotion(s) and choose actions from a centered place. Participate with Effectiveness and respond rather than react.

Results: Observe and Describe what results from the emotion and actions (or inactions). Evaluate what worked and what did not work. Learn from your experience. Emotions and choices in response to feelings influence what happens with subsequent events. Use this knowledge to continue positive emotions with Mood Momentum or break out of ineffective emotions with Opposite to Emotion.

FEELINGS MODEL APPLICATION

Core concept: Use this worksheet to discover how emotions (and emotional patterns) happen.

Describe the **Event** (What happened; who, what, when, and where?):

Describe your **Interpretation** (What judgment, evaluation, self-talk, or belief was activated?):

Describe your **Feeling** (What is happening physically? What is the body language? Put a name on the emotion, using a feeling chart if needed. Identify underlying feelings, too, if possible.):

Describe your **Action Urge** (What is the emotional pull toward an action, inaction, or communication? Would it fit Wise Mind? This is a moment of CHOICE.):

Describe your **Action** (What action or inaction can be made? Participate Effectively.):

Describe the **Results** (What consequences occurred? Include other emotions, thoughts, actions and inactions, and their effect on relationships and situations. How did the results set up the next event (e.g., did a pattern continue or did the cycle change)?:

Basic Feelings and Their Opposites

Core concept: Feelings have opposites and can exist on a dialectic.

Following is a list of basic feelings and their opposites. Start to think about and discuss feelings to gain a better understanding.

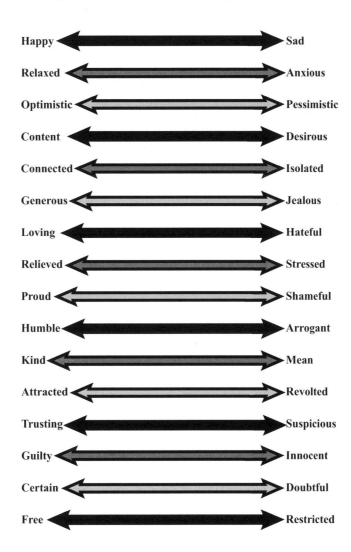

Happy	Sad
Relaxed	Anxious
Optimistic	Pessimistic
Content	Desirous
Connected	Isolated
Generous	Jealous
Loving	Hateful
Relieved	Stressed
Proud	Shameful
Humble	Arrogant
Kind	Mean
Attracted	Revolted
Trusting	Suspicious
Guilty	Innocent
Certain	Doubtful
Free	Restricted

We use Mood Momentum to continue or increase the feelings we want to keep around and Opposite to Emotion to decrease the feelings we want to change.

Feelings on a Continuum

Core concept: Identify lower intensities of an emotion for early intervention.

Feelings come with different intensity levels. Use Observe and Describe to notice lower-intensity feelings for early and proactive skill use. We can use Mindfulness to attend to our feelings and Opposite to Emotion to get unstuck from negative emotions. These approaches work best at lower emotional levels. We can also use Mood Momentum to prolong and increase positive emotions.

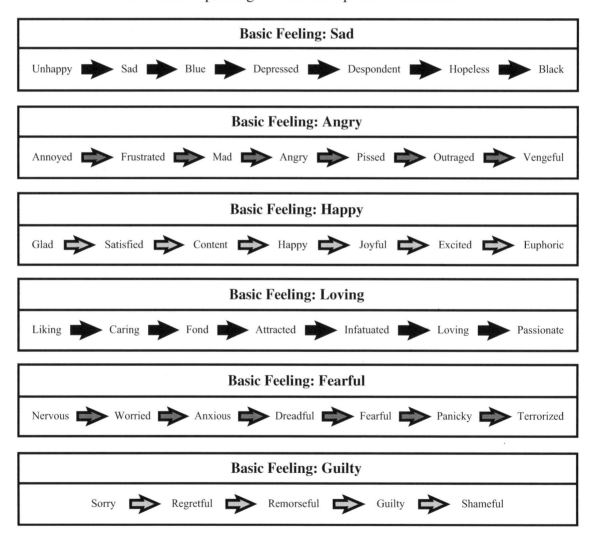

Basic Feeling: Sad

Unhappy → Sad → Blue → Depressed → Despondent → Hopeless → Black

Basic Feeling: Angry

Annoyed → Frustrated → Mad → Angry → Pissed → Outraged → Vengeful

Basic Feeling: Happy

Glad → Satisfied → Content → Happy → Joyful → Excited → Euphoric

Basic Feeling: Loving

Liking → Caring → Fond → Attracted → Infatuated → Loving → Passionate

Basic Feeling: Fearful

Nervous → Worried → Anxious → Dreadful → Fearful → Panicky → Terrorized

Basic Feeling: Guilty

Sorry → Regretful → Remorseful → Guilty → Shameful

Remember that we can rate any feeling on a continuum from 1 to 10 (low to high) or simply observe it as low, medium, or high. Also remember that we Observe and Describe feelings with Nonjudgmental Stance to avoid adding to or intensifying them.

Changing Your Relationship to Feelings

Core concept: Making an attempt to understand feelings changes our relationship to them.

Emotions are not good, bad, right, or wrong. The first step to changing our relationship to feelings is to become curious about them and use Nonjudgmental Stance. What purpose do they serve?

Feelings exist so we can connect and relate to other people and create meaningful relationships. Our feelings allow us to share joy and love with those around us and to be compassionate and empathic with others. Our emotions also communicate very quickly to people around us without needing words.

Emotions motivate us not only in relationships but also in other aspects of life. Often, feelings provide us with intuitive information that motivates our behavior without our thought. This emotional guidance can be highly effective in certain situations. It can even enable us to overcome seemingly impossible obstacles.

When our emotions seem to cloud our lives, such as when we are depressed or anxious or angry, it is important to remember that those emotions are still giving us important information. Rather than judging our emotions, we want to practice acceptance of them and open our minds to listen to their messages. When we reject feelings or try to "get rid" of them, it often has the effect of intensifying them; the message is not getting through, so it needs to get louder.

We notice that when others invalidate our emotions, the feelings get more intense. Self-invalidation has the same effect.

Practice nonjudgmental acceptance of your feelings and listen to their message. Also, remember that emotions are not facts, and that a healthy relationship to feelings comes from Wise Mind.

Mindfully "Hold" Feelings to Soothe and Reduce Suffering

Core concept: Mindfulness of our feelings can soothe them.

We add suffering to emotional pain when we try to get rid of, fight, or judge our feelings. Like any rejection, these approaches create a negative counter-response. Our feelings are a part of us with information to share, and the refusal to accept them turns up their intensity.

Willingness to be with our feelings soothes them. It is like truly listening to a concern from another or sitting with someone's distress without having to fix it. *Not* fixing your feelings and being mindful of them is a solution. Even strong emotions do not require action.

Similar to Urge Surfing, we "hold" our emotions through Mindfulness. Holding feelings means that we recognize them as a part of experience but not who we are as people. When we simply *be* with our emotions, we open ourselves to their ebbs and flows nonjudgmentally and find that the intensity usually subsides.

Observe your emotions without getting stuck, and practice Radical Acceptance when they are painful. If you find yourself overwhelmed, change strategies and use Distress Tolerance skills.

You will find that emotions have important information for you, and they soothe themselves when we listen to them. Acceptance in the moment frees you from the grip your feelings have on you.

Build Positive Experience (BPE)

Core concept: Positive events create positive feelings.

Feelings such as happiness do not just happen. They are a byproduct of what we think and what we do. Positive events and thinking build positive feelings. As straightforward as this concept seems, it can be difficult to put into action.

Many of us lack interest and energy, and these barriers can prevent positive events. The result is that positive emotions will remain unlikely. Interest, enjoyment, and energy will eventually follow positive events, especially if we invest in the experience without a strong desire or need to control the outcome. Let positive emotions happen organically.

Sometimes we feel like we do not deserve positive experiences, worry about expectations, or dread the end of a positive experience. Treat these issues like distractions and use Mindfulness to focus on the positive experiences.

Other barriers to using Build Positive Experience exist, too. Take a moment to look at your barriers.

Describe your barriers to using Build Positive Experience:

Describe the skills you will use to address each barrier:

We can think of using Build Positive Experience in a few ways. We have positive experiences that are possible right now, positive experiences that we can plan and look forward to in the short-term and positive experiences that we work toward step-by-step in the long term.

Positive Events Right Now: What can be a positive event in the here and now or immediate future? Maybe it is a conversation, hearing or telling a joke, or helping someone. It might be taking a break (see Vacation), taking a quick walk, or taking a few minutes to practice mindfulness. You may find that the positive event is simply soaking in some sunshine, seeing rain wash everything clean, or feeling a warm breeze.

There are an enormous number of positive events possible now. We just need to turn our minds toward them and be open to the experience with our full attention.

Positive Events Planned in the Short Term: These positive events can include a regular family meal, an outing alone or with a friend, a Friday movie night, or anything you can plan and schedule over the short term.

Start by listing your interests, hobbies, and activities you like to do (or used to do) and add activities to try from the Activities List. If you have a short list, you may have to develop some additional interests through trying out a lot of new activities with an open mind. Plan time for these positive events in your schedule and follow through with them. (See ROUTINE and Opposite to Emotion)

Short-term positive events need to be regular occurrences and planned daily to be effective. Having regular positive events to look forward to moves you toward a satisfying life.

If interest and energy are low, it may take weeks to experience the benefits. Do not give up on the process or get into judgments about not getting the desired outcomes right away.

Participating in the journey will eventually get you to the destination.

Positive Events to Work Toward in the Long Term: Make a list of your long-term priorities and goals. It may be going to school, learning a craft, making a career change, taking up an instrument, being in great physical shape, or having a vision for making a difference in the world.

Pick something from your list and break it down into manageable steps. Plan and schedule time to work on that first step, and follow through on it. (See ROUTINE and Opposite to Emotion) As you accomplish each step, give yourself credit and plan the next step. A thousand-mile journey starts with a single step.

Your work toward long-term positives is a major part of building a satisfying life. Remember that some steps can be hard or frustrating. Do not give up, and stay focused on what you want in the long term.

Positive Event Planning, Scheduling, and Your Routine: You may not know what to do to Build Positive Experience or how to plan these experiences. As stated earlier, first, you should identify possible positive experiences and schedule them, or they are less likely to happen. (See Activities List and ROUTINE) Then you have to follow through with your plan using Opposite to Emotion when needed.

Mindfulness and Positive Events: Using Build Positive Experience requires your Mindfulness skills to be effective. Stay focused on the event and not when it will end, how expectations might change, or anything else that could take away from the experience.

Describe how your life will be different when you effectively use Build Positive Experience:

Attend to Relationships (A2R)

Core concept: Tending to relationships creates positive feelings.

Life events, problems, and symptoms can disrupt our relationships. We may have neglected friends and family or have simply lost track of those connections. At other times, we may have actively damaged relationships or burned others out with our struggles. We may be lonely, and isolation tends to create and maintain unwanted feelings.

Attending to Relationships is a way to Build Positive Experience that tends to create positive feelings over time. When you use this skill, remember to also use Interpersonal Effectiveness, BOUNDARIES, Nonjudgmental Stance, and Opposite to Emotion.

Start with two lists of people: those who are currently in your life and those from the past who you would want in your life again. Only list people with whom you have or had a positive connection with overall. *Do not list unhealthy people or people with whom you have had hopeless relationships.*

These people are in my life now:

Describe how you can better attend to each person and how you can repair relationships if needed:

These are people from my past with whom I would like to be reconnected:

Describe how you can reconnect with at least one person on this list, how you can attend to that person, and how you can repair the relationship if needed:

If you find that your lists are short, you are not alone. Many of us need new people in our lives for a lot of different reasons; start thinking about making new relationships.

Describe your resources and places where you might reach out for new relationships:

Describe the other skills you will use to start making new relationships:

Describe how your life will be different when you effectively use Attend to Relationships:

Describe how you will acknowledge and celebrate having healthier relationships:

Mood Momentum (MM)

Core concept: Notice positive moods and choose skills to keep them going.

We influence feelings with the behaviors we choose. When we Observe and Describe an emotion that we want to continue to experience, we can use Mood Momentum. This skill directs us to stay involved in events and thoughts that keep our positive emotions around so we can benefit from the momentum of already feeling well.

Emotions tend to unconsciously draw us to behaviors that are congruent or fit with them. Mood Momentum is a mindful effort to choose these mood-congruent behaviors when they will be helpful. Ways to continue positive moods include the following:

- Engage in using Build Positive Experience
- Balance using Build Positive Experience with using Build Mastery
- Use Mindfulness to reflect on a positive emotion
- Engage in using PLEASED
- Balance active positive events with relaxing positive events
- Engage in healthy relationships
- Work on a responsibility and stay mindful of your efforts and accomplishments (and distract from judgments)
- Practice Mindfulness exercises
- Work on a hobby or project or try something on the Activities List
- Think of other ways you can use Mood Momentum

A key to Mood Momentum is to pick from a variety of positive experiences, activities, and behaviors to keep it interesting. Even the most fun or relaxing event will eventually reach the point where it no longer creates a positive effect. We benefit most from Mood Momentum when we take a balanced approach, switch up our strategies, and keep it fresh.

Opposite to Emotion (O2E)

Core concept: Use opposite action to get unstuck from negative emotions.

We get stuck in difficult feelings partly due to mood-congruent behavior. Mood-congruent behavior occurs when, without awareness, we fall into behavior patterns that keep our negative emotions around. For example, when we feel depressed, we may perform the following actions (or fail to act in the following ways):

- Getting isolated (e.g., being disconnected from relationships, not answering the phone, missing social engagements and appointments)
- Being inactive (e.g., staying in bed or on the couch, not participating in hobbies or potentially positive experiences, letting the chores at home and other responsibilities pile up)
- Engaging in stuck thinking (e.g., focusing only on the negative, ruminating, wanting to die)
- Neglecting self-care and hygiene
- Eating and sleeping too much or too little
- Deciding to stop therapy and medications
- Engaging in other behaviors that perpetuate negative emotional states

Unfortunately, these automatic reactions to depression keep us depressed and may even make it worse. This is where Opposite to Emotion (also known as Opposite Action) is helpful. This dialectical skill directs us to act in ways that are the opposite of the behaviors toward which our difficult emotions pull us. For the depressive examples just given, we would use Opposite to Emotion to:

- Reach out to relationships for help and positive experience.
- Get moving by doing activities, hobbies, and important tasks. Use ROUTINE, the Activities List, Build Positive Experience, Build Mastery, or engage in Distress Tolerance skills.
- Practice MIDDLE Cs, take a Nonjudgmental Stance, or use Encouragement.
- Use PLEASED.

- Go to therapy appointments and discuss medication issues with your prescriber before making changes.
- Use other skills to address additional behaviors that perpetuate negative emotional states.

See the following explanations and examples for ways to use Opposite Action to address common difficult emotions.

Opposite to Emotion with Anxiety or Fear: We tend to avoid when we feel anxiety and fear. We also tend to ruminate on anxious thoughts. Avoidance gets reinforced because it helps us protect ourselves from distress. However, the more we avoid, the more our anxieties build over time, and we end up feeling more overwhelmed. In addition, avoidance results in our world getting smaller and smaller.

Using Opposite Action means approaching our fears one step at a time and learning to tolerate the distress that comes with it. To do this effectively, we use mindfulness to desensitize ourselves and Distress Tolerance when we feel too overwhelmed. The more we approach rather than avoid, the more our nervous system learns to be "bored," and the less anxious we feel.

We can also learn to accept our anxious thoughts rather than fight them or catastrophize about them. This approach takes the power out of the thoughts.

Opposite to Emotion with Anger: We often want to lash out with words or behavior when we feel anger, and we may replay the situation over and over in our minds. Using Opposite Action can include being kind and compassionate to others. We can spend quality time with our pets and children, being careful to be gentle and not to displace our anger.

Alternatively, we might imagine compassion for someone we feel anger toward (which is difficult to do sometimes). Remember that most people (including ourselves) do not want to make mistakes and do not want others to be angry at them, no matter how unskillfully they act. Compassion can be dialectically balanced with accountability.

Distract from angry thoughts by using the Thoughts skill. Count to 100 or recite the alphabet. Focus on thoughts that are the opposite of angry thoughts. Use MIDDLE Cs.

Do not stuff anger, because this sets the stage for rage. When anger is at a workable level, see if it fits Wise Mind and use Interpersonal Effectiveness if needed.

Opposite to Emotion with Guilt and Shame: We feel guilt when we have done something to hurt ourselves or others or when we make mistakes. Often we try to avoid or hide from others when we feel guilt, or we try to blame or otherwise avoid accepting responsibility for our actions.

Using Opposite Action means addressing what we did or the mistake that we made with whoever was affected. We apologize and try to make the situation better if possible. If we cannot make the situation better, then we try to do something better somewhere; this is a symbolic way to "right" a "wrong." Be committed to not repeating the same mistakes and develop a plan to act differently in the future.

A genuine apology is for the benefit of the other person and not a means for avoiding consequences. Others still may be upset for a time after your apology. Be patient with the process. Accept consequences with grace unless they do not fit the situation as evaluated in Wise Mind. Do not participate in guilt or consequences that are out of proportion with the situation.

After you have completed the steps listed here, let go of the situation and the thoughts that caused the guilt. Use Radical Acceptance.

Sometimes guilt does *not* fit Wise Mind. For example, we have a right to say no and to have boundaries; we do not need to feel guilty for exerting this right. At other times, we experience guilt in the absence of wrongdoing for a variety of reasons. Examples include feeling guilty for practicing Self-soothe skills, for having a good time, or for taking time for ourselves. This type of guilt leads us to avoid behaviors like saying no, setting boundaries, and participating in beneficial activities.

When we have guilt that does not fit Wise Mind, the Opposite Action is to approach rather than avoid. Keep practicing saying no, setting boundaries, and participating in activities until you no longer feel guilty. Remember to use REASON, MIDDLE Cs, and Encouragement with your thoughts that prompt guilt.

We feel shame when guilt is not addressed, when we have done something serious, or when something serious has happened to us. Shame involves having judgments about being damaged, unlovable, or unforgivable.

We can also feel shame for how we look or who we are as people even when it does not fit Wise Mind. This type of shame frequently originates from others' judgments and from being mistreated. Shame causes us to hide, and hiding keeps the shame around.

Using Opposite Action with shame involves coming out of hiding and talking about what causes us shame with *someone safe, nonjudgmental, and accepting*. As we work through shame, we can often open ourselves up to more and more supportive people and begin to heal. The process of working through shame also requires a Nonjudgmental Stance and Distress Tolerance skills.

OPPOSITE TO EMOTION (O2E) APPLICATION

Core concept: Use this worksheet to practice opposite action.

Describe your current feeling:

Describe what actions (or inactions) this feeling is pulling you to do (what is mood congruent?):

Describe the predicted outcomes from these actions (or inactions):

Describe how you can use Opposite Action:

Describe the predicted outcomes from your use of Opposite Action:

Describe how your life will be different when you effectively use Opposite Action:

Describe how you will acknowledge and celebrate your effective use of Opposite Action:

Building a Satisfying Life

Core concept: Routines and structure will build your satisfying life.

Every life is worth living, but many of us find our lives unsatisfying, unenjoyable, or even miserable at times. Life is more satisfying when we develop routines that include predictable and enjoyable relaxation and fun balanced with responsibilities.

Routines do not need to be complicated. In fact, most of us benefit from mindful simplicity in life. Mindful simplicity means connecting to and experiencing the routines that define and structure our days.

Consider that the Dalai Lama (2009) describes a daily routine that includes meals, meditation, studying scripture, mending watches, gardening, working, and watching a little TV before bed. Our routines do not have to be spectacular. Peace and enjoyment can come with predictability.

Also consider that what works for children generally works for adults. Many of us make the mistake in believing that we no longer need the structure and predictability that children do. In some cases, we never had structure or predictability as children, so we never had the opportunity to continue having it in adolescence or adulthood.

One of the first tasks of building a satisfying life is establishing a routine. Before beginning, consider the following dialectic: *want to* versus *have to*. Our routines need balance between what we want to do and what we have to do, and we need to have a middle ground between enjoyable activities and responsibilities. Dialectically speaking, going too far in either direction creates the need for balance with the opposite. We need to rework our routine when we are stuck on one side versus the other.

Two other dialectics to consider include *structure* versus *flexibility* and *predictability* versus *novelty*. Remember that structured routines benefit us, but if they get too rigid, we may feel trapped by them. Obviously, the other extreme of excessive flexibility may result in too much unpredictability or chaos, which stands in the way of developing a satisfying life.

Too much flexibility leaves us unsure about what we need to be doing, and that causes distress. The middle ground is creating a routine that is solid but includes opportunity for change and flexibility based on the demands of the day.

A predictable routine allows us to feel settled and safe and to have a "home base" from which to operate. At the same time, too much predictability leads to feeling stifled. We also need to experience novelty and change in our routines. Every day does not need to be the same. Planning open times and free days can be part of establishing the balance.

Remember that building a routine will take time, but will reap great rewards.

Using ROUTINE (RO)

Core concept: Develop a schedule to get your life on track.

Use the acronym *ROUTINE* to remember the building blocks (**R**esponsibilities, **O**ngoing Structure, **U**se of Skills, **T**raditions, **I**nterests Included, **N**ovelty, **E**nvision a Satisfying Life) of this skill. These building blocks are described in further detail in the paragraphs that follow.

Responsibilities: We get overwhelmed when our responsibilities are not taken care of daily. Break bigger responsibilities down into daily steps. Make a list of both major and minor responsibilities and fill them into the "Schedule" worksheet.

Ongoing Structure: Routines are about structure that is ongoing, predictable, and repeating. Structure keeps us from getting stuck in symptoms and is the foundation for building a satisfying life. Use the "Schedule" worksheet to structure your days and be sure to follow it.

Use of Skills: Remember that you need to learn and practice all of your skills as a part of your routine, just like someone in school or college does daily homework. Include reminders for the skills you want to specifically practice on a given day. Also remember that other skills might be needed to follow your routine, like Opposite to Emotion.

Traditions: Traditions give meaning to our lives and those of others. Part of a satisfying life is developing traditions that you and the people around you enjoy.

Many of us think of traditions as being tied to seasons and holidays (and those can be fun to establish), but traditions can also be as simple as a family bowling night, a specific dinner on a certain night, or celebrating accomplishments (yours or others) with something special. You can get back into traditions you have valued or use your imagination to create new traditions for yourself and your loved ones.

Interests Included: Routines that do not include our personal interests are difficult to maintain. Be sure to build in what you like to do. If you are unsure what you are interested in, pick some options from the Activities List and plug them into your schedule. Remember to approach a new interest or activity with a Nonjudgmental Stance.

<u>N</u>ovelty: Be careful not to build too much structure into your routine. Routines also need space for flexibility and novelty. Make sure you explicitly leave space to try new activities or be spontaneous. Consider "scheduling" a free morning, afternoon, evening, or day into your routine.

<u>E</u>nvision a Satisfying Life: Routines, schedules, and structure take time to get established. Remember not to give up on building habits toward living a more satisfying life. Stay mindful of how your routine will help you with your priorities, goals, and values. Do not give up!

Everyday Care

Core concept: Basic physical and mental care need to be part of a daily routine.

Basic physical and mental self-care is needed every day to establish a foundation on which to build. (See Well-being) As we learn more skills, we might develop (or you may already have developed) more elaborate and effective self-care. For most of us, we need to revisit the basics at least occasionally.

Refer to the lists that follow and then describe the other tasks you would like to attend to each day.

ROUTINE PHYSICAL SELF-CARE:

- Brush teeth
- Wash face and/or bathe or shower
- Put on clean clothes
- Take medications, vitamins, etc.
- Eat a balanced meal at least three times a day plus healthy snacks
- Move around, stretch, and exercise
- Have a bedtime routine
- Perform other physical self-care tasks

Describe other routine **physical** self-care tasks you need daily:

ROUTINE MENTAL SELF-CARE:

- Mindfulness (breathing or relaxation)
- Identify positives and gratefulness
- Encourage yourself
- Plan positive activities
- Connect with family, friends, and support
- Nurture your spirit
- Perform other mental self-care tasks

Describe other routine **mental** self-care tasks you need daily:

Describe how your life will be different when you effectively practice physical and mental self-care:

Describe how you will acknowledge and celebrate your physical and mental self-care efforts:

Activities List

We need to have pleasant activities scheduled every day. Below is a list of pleasant activities, many of which are free. Add specific pleasant activities to the list that you enjoy. Make sure to schedule at least three pleasant activities each day. Also, remember to use Mindfulness skills with each experience.

1. Dress up or down
2. Play board games
3. Have a snack mindfully
4. Appreciate a favorite actor or act yourself
5. Read the Bible or other religious text
6. Advocate for the National Alliance on Mental Illness (NAMI), a political cause, or the environment
7. Stargaze, find constellations, or wonder about the universe
8. Read about animals or visit the zoo
9. Appreciate the arts or create your own
10. Play badminton
11. Redecorate or rearrange your house
12. Join a group
13. Have a conversation with a friend or a stranger
14. Watch or play baseball or softball
15. Make crafts
16. Watch, read about, or fly an airplane or build a model
17. Watch or play basketball or play HORSE
18. Bathe or shower mindfully
19. Relax at (or imagine being at) the beach; look for shells or clean the beach up
20. Do beadwork
21. Beatbox, rap, or sing
22. Ring a bell
23. Breathe mindfully
24. Write a short story
25. Bike
26. Feed or watch birds
27. Blog or visit blogs
28. Boat
29. Bowl
30. Bet a small amount of money
31. Start a fantasy football league (or join one)
32. Play checkers
33. Help the disabled
34. Contribute at a food pantry
35. Bake a cake and decorate it

36. Go geocaching
37. Do calligraphy
38. Camp
39. Make candles or ice candles
40. Canoe
41. Have a picnic in your home
42. Read about cars or go for a drive
43. Do some cheerleading
44. Take a nap
45. Watch one television show mindfully
46. Window-shop (without spending)
47. Play chess
48. Go to church and associated activities
49. Watch clouds
50. Make a sand castle
51. Collect coins
52. Go to an antique shop to browse
53. Collect artwork
54. Collect albums or CDs or look at and listen to old ones
55. Compose music or lyrics
56. Look at architecture in magazines or around town
57. Enjoy perfume or cologne
58. Do computer activities
59. Cook
60. Crochet
61. Cross-stitch
62. Do a crossword puzzle
63. Dance anywhere
64. Play darts (not lawn darts)
65. Look at your collectibles
66. Bowl with friends or in a league
67. Daydream
68. Juggle
69. Play dominoes or set them up to let them fall
70. Draw
71. Eat out or fix a special meal at home
72. Take a community education course or educate yourself on a new topic
73. Tinker with electronics
74. Do embroidery
75. Entertain others
76. Exercise: aerobics, weights, yoga
77. Go fishing
78. Watch or play football
79. Take a hot or cool shower
80. Tell jokes and laugh
81. Go four-wheeling
82. Paint a wall
83. Enjoy or maintain an aquarium
84. Play Frisbee® or disc golf
85. Mend clothes
86. Have a spirited debate (without needing to be right)
87. Join a club
88. Play games
89. Garden
90. Swim
91. Keep a dream journal
92. Hug a friend or family member
93. Visit garage sales

94. Be intimate with a loved one
95. Be a mentor
96. Build a bird house
97. Do genealogy
98. Walk your (or a neighbor's) dog
99. Visit an art museum
100. Go to the movies or watch a favorite DVD
101. Golf
102. Practice putting
103. Give yourself a facial
104. Paint a picture or finger-paint
105. Watch funny YouTube® videos (or post one)
106. Find an activity listed more than once on this list
107. Go go-kart racing
108. Play Texas Hold 'Em
109. Volunteer at the Humane Society
110. Write a letter to the editor
111. Light a candle and enjoy the smell or the flame
112. Play video games
113. Scrapbook
114. Become a pen pal
115. Support any cause
116. Play guitar
117. Write a handwritten letter
118. Hike
119. Do home repair
120. Breath in fresh air
121. Build a home theater system
122. Record your favorite shows and watch back to back
123. Air drum or air guitar to a cool song
124. Ride a horse
125. Write a thank you letter
126. Hunt
127. Surf the Internet
128. Fix a bike
129. Make jewelry
130. Browse your favorite store
131. Put together a jigsaw puzzle
132. Build a fort with your kids
133. Journal
134. Juggle
135. Kayak
136. See life like a young child
137. Say a prayer
138. Build or fly kites
139. Knit
140. Tie knots
141. Sing a silly song
142. Pick flowers
143. Learn anything new
144. Learn a foreign language
145. Practice telling a joke
146. Learn an instrument
147. Listen to music
148. Macramé
149. Color with kids (or without)
150. Smile at someone
151. Be affectionate
152. Do a magic trick
153. Meditate
154. Use a metal detector
155. Teach a child something
156. Build models
157. Ride or look at motorcycles
158. Play with children

159. Go mountain biking
160. Work with a team
161. Plant an herb garden
162. Go to a community center
163. Grow a Chia® pet
164. Climb a mountain
165. Make a root beer float
166. Lie in the grass
167. Scrapbook
168. Practice a musical instrument
169. Needlepoint
170. Read reviews on a topic of interest
171. Do origami
172. Play Trivial Pursuit® or any trivia game
173. Clean out a closet and donate unneeded items
174. Plan a movie marathon
175. Look at StumbleUpon.com
176. Join a chat room
177. Play paintball
178. Go to a water park
179. Pass on something thoughtful found on the Internet
180. Go to a video arcade
181. Indulge in a guilty pleasure
182. Email friends and family
183. Join a drum circle
184. Rollerblade
185. Swing at a playground
186. Go to the mall to walk or browse (without spending)
187. Water your plants
188. Make a collage
189. Hang with a friend
190. Listen to music and read the lyrics
191. Try a new recipe
192. Paint your nails
193. Sit by any body of water
194. Go to the library
195. Organize a neighborhood garden
196. Groom a pet
197. Watch a sunrise or sunset
198. Take a walk
199. Go the a health club or YMCA
200. Go to a coffee shop

List the activities you like (or have liked) to do:

Circle at least 10 new activities from the list that you are willing to try.

Describe how your life will be different when you schedule and involve yourself in activities:

My Routines and Schedule

Core concept: Develop your routines and daily schedule.

Directions: Develop a routine by filling out a schedule weekly (you will need to get a calendar, ideally a daily planner). Begin by scheduling regular wake and sleep times and fill in the hours in between starting with your non-negotiable appointments and obligations. Then, fill in times for self-care and positive activities.

Use the ROUTINE acronym, the Everyday Care section, and the Activities List to outline the days in a typical week for you. Also, consult the Smaller Routines Application worksheet that follows this section for other ideas.

Follow your schedule and fine-tune it weekly based on what works and what needs change. Remember that mindfully following a balanced and predictable routine will be a huge step toward building a satisfying life.

Day Of The Week: _____	
Time	**Activity**

SMALLER ROUTINES APPLICATION

Core concept: Develop small routines that reap big benefits.

Start to develop smaller routines in life and be consistent with what works. Note the examples, but be sure to individualize your routines. Be sure you make time for these smaller routines in your daily schedule above. Also remember to practice Mindfulness with your routines.

Describe your morning routine (e.g., get up, take medications, use bathroom, make tea, eat breakfast, shower/bathe, journal, meditate/relax, prepare to leave or transition to next routine):

Describe your work (school, volunteering, etc.) routine (e.g., arrive, get organized, listen to voicemail and check emails, check in with coworkers, set goals for the day, get started):

Describe your evening routine (e.g., check mail and complete tasks, make dinner and eat, clean up kitchen, socialize, read, watch TV, and relax):

Describe your bedtime routine (e.g., brush teeth, wash face, put on pajamas, lay out clothes for tomorrow, write down positives and gratefulness and goals for tomorrow, practice mindfulness and relaxation):

Describe other smaller routines (e.g., leisure, relaxation, etc.) that are important to you:

Describe how your life will be different when you effectively and mindfully follow routines and schedules:

Describe how you will acknowledge and celebrate your effective use of routines and schedules:

Boundaries (BO)

Core concept: Boundaries keep relationships healthy and safe.

Boundaries exist to define who we are separate from others. A goal in relationships is to be in healthy contact with others without getting too enmeshed or being too disconnected.

It is important to be connected with others while also maintaining our own emotional, psychological, and physical space. Boundaries are dialectical in nature, as we strive to balance our interpersonal needs and comfort zones with those of others.

Healthy boundaries help us to have meaningful relationships without taking on others' distress and problems and without being isolated and alone. Boundaries define who we are as individuals in relation to others and the world.

Like types of fences (e.g., invisible versus picket versus barbed wire), boundaries vary based on the context of situations, settings, and how defined we need to be in relation to others. Our experience, what we Observe and Describe, and our priorities, goals, and values inform us about what type of fences to put up.

It is difficult to recognize and practice healthy boundaries if others have not modeled them in our lives. The lack of healthy models for boundaries results in difficulties in relationships that in turn decrease self-respect.

The BOUNDARIES module defines different types of boundaries and outlines a model to establish and maintain boundaries based in values and safety.

It is important to know that factors like personality, family, culture, locale, situation, and setting (among other factors) influence boundaries. Boundaries are complex.

Definitions and Types of Boundaries

Core concept: Define boundaries in order to practice them.

Physical: Physical boundaries include your body and the space that surrounds it (i.e. your personal space). Physical boundaries can be defined by who is allowed to touch us and in what areas. These boundaries include all levels of physical intimacy and sexual practices. Additionally, physical boundaries include what goes into us, like food and drink, or anything else that affects our physical being.

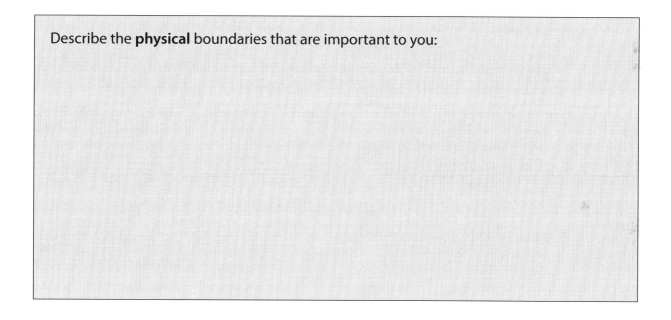

Describe the **physical** boundaries that are important to you:

Psychological: Psychological boundaries include information about yourself, your thoughts and beliefs, and your values. These boundaries might include topics of conversation and anything that occupies your "mental" space. Who knows about your inner life and how it is shared (if at all) constitute psychological boundary issues.

Describe the **psychological** boundaries that are important to you:

Emotional: Emotional boundaries include your feelings and their ability to be leveraged and manipulated (e.g., emotional "hostage taking" or guilt-tripping). Emotional boundaries also include not taking on others' distress (or expecting them to take on yours). Like psychological boundaries, who knows about your feelings and how they are shared (if at all) constitute emotional boundary issues.

Describe the **emotional** boundaries that are important to you:

Spiritual: Spiritual boundaries include your ability to choose your own religion, higher power, or spiritual life (or lack thereof). Who knows about your spiritual life and how it is shared (if at all) constitute spiritual boundary issues.

Describe the **spiritual** boundaries that are important to you:

General: Anything that defines and differentiates you as separate from others (and others from you) is a boundary, and anything needed to keep you healthy and "safe" interpersonally and in the world constitutes a boundary issue.

Describe **general** boundaries that are important to you:

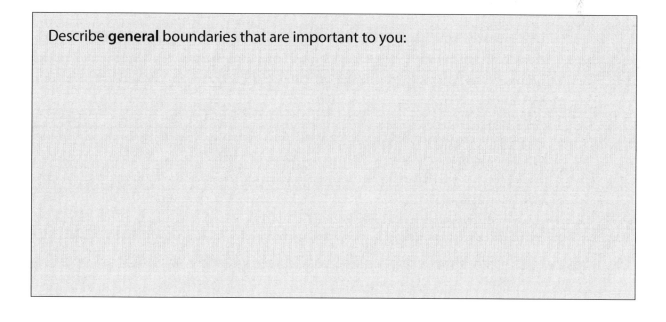

Using BOUNDARY (BO)

Core concept: This skill helps us to define and maintain boundaries.

Use the acronym *BOUNDARY* to remember the building blocks (**B**e Aware of Self, **O**bserve Others and the Situation, **U**nderstand Your and Others' Limits, **N**egotiate Sometimes, **D**ifferences Exist, **A**lways **R**emember Your Values, **Y**our Safety Comes First) of this skill. These building blocks are described in further detail in the paragraphs that follow.

Be Aware of Self: Use Observe and Describe to notice what you are sharing and what you are doing. Does your behavior fit the situation and your relationships with others? Does your behavior feel comfortable? Notice if your boundaries are at either extreme, being too closed or too open for the situation and the relationships.

Observe Others and the Situation: What is happening in the situation and with others? Notice the level of interest, the information shared, and the behavior of others. Does the sharing and the behavior of others seem healthy and respectful? Observe and Describe what you are sharing and doing in the context of others. Understand that your boundaries exist in relation to those of others.

Understand Your and Others' Limits: We all have important boundaries or limits. Be aware of your boundaries and maintain them from Wise Mind based on the needs of the situation and the relationships between you and others. Also be aware of others' boundaries and respect them.

Negotiate Sometimes: In important relationships, we sometimes negotiate our boundaries. Negotiations happen from Wise Mind and rarely involve extreme changes. Avoid negotiating boundaries in unimportant relationships, in new relationships, or to be liked. Put your self-respect above being liked by others.

You may also negotiate your boundaries if there is a benefit in adjusting them. If your boundaries can be too undefined, work on tighter limits. If your boundaries can be too rigid, work on more flexible limits. Again, make adjustments from Wise Mind.

Differences Exist: Negotiating boundaries is effective at times, but we need to balance negotiations with a healthy respect for individual differences, too. Differences in boundaries happen due to personality, personal history, culture, situations, settings, and for other reasons. Sometimes it is not about negotiating boundaries but maintaining your boundaries while being respectful of others' boundaries. Use Radical Acceptance or Everyday Acceptance with individual differences and learn not to take those differences "personally" (this is a boundary, too).

Always Remember Your Values: The decision to negotiate and adjust your boundaries or to maintain them needs to be grounded in your priorities, goals, and values. Use your values as a compass to guide your boundaries and do not compromise boundaries at the expense of self-respect.

Your Safety Comes First: People sometimes compromise boundaries to be liked or to fit in with others. Avoid situations that can harm you emotionally, psychologically, physically, or spiritually.

BOUNDARIES (BO) APPLICATION

Core concept: Use this worksheet to define boundaries.

Describe your **physical** boundaries:

Describe your **psychological** boundaries:

Describe your **emotional** boundaries:

Describe your **spiritual** boundaries:

Describe **general** boundary issues important to you:

Describe what boundaries may be negotiable in some situations:

Describe what boundaries will be non-negotiable to you:

Describe how establishing and maintaining boundaries can build and maintain your self-respect:

Describe how your life will be different when you establish and maintain effective boundaries:

Describe how you will acknowledge and celebrate healthy boundaries in your relationships:

Interpersonal Effectiveness

Core concept: Interpersonal skills lead to healthy relationships.

Interpersonal Effectiveness skills enable us to make and maintain relationships, resolve conflict when it occurs, and get our and others' wants and needs met effectively in a balanced manner.

This module has three main sets of skills: FAST, GIVE, and DEAR MAN. FAST skills build self-respect. You have a relationship with yourself. The way that you talk to yourself and the behaviors you choose affect how you feel about yourself. FAST skills orient us to make choices and act in relationships in ways that increase our self-respect. Self-respect is based in actions grounded in our priorities, goals, and values. Respecting yourself provides the foundation for skill use in your relationships with others.

GIVE skills are other-focused. We want to treat others with care, interest, validation, and respect. This approach allows us to form and nurture meaningful relationships that will enrich our lives. GIVE also enables us to be dialectic in conflicts so we can resolve them effectively.

DEAR MAN is assertiveness that is self-focused. We use DEAR MAN to get our wants and needs met more reliably, to say no, to set boundaries with others, and to negotiate when needed. DEAR MAN also involves skills that build our confidence and competence.

We use all three sets of skills to be effective in our relationships. Remember to role-play and practice these skills consistently.

Interpersonal Effectiveness and Dialectics

Core concept: Relationships require balance and working the middle ground.

Dialectics are central to healthy relationships. Being too other-focused or too self-focused leads to unmet wants and needs and conflict. Instead, we attempt to find balance in relationships, and that balance differs based on with whom we are interacting along with the context of the situation.

Think of GIVE and DEAR MAN existing on a dialectic:

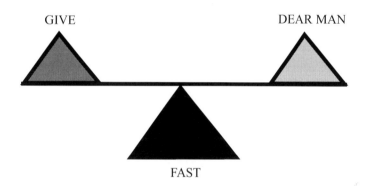

At times we need to focus on others and at other times we need to focus on ourselves. In practice, we are most effective when we blend both sets of skills. The blend between thinking about others versus ourselves is grounded in FAST. We use our values to guide us in relationships to enhance our self-respect and others' respect for us.

Ask yourself three questions when working the dialectic in relationships:

1. What does the other person need in this interaction (GIVE)?

2. What do I need in this interaction (DEAR MAN)?

3. What is needed in this interaction to maintain or build my self-respect (FAST)?

Using FAST (F)

Core concept: Self-respect and healthy relationships start with you.

FAST skills are focused on our priorities, goals, and values so we can make choices that build our self-respect. Self-respect is the foundation to liking ourselves, and it creates a solid base for us to build and maintain relationships with others.

Use the acronym *FAST* to remember the building blocks (**F**air, **A**pologies Not Needed, **S**tick to Values, **T**ruth and Accountability) of this skill. These building blocks are described in further detail in the paragraphs that follow.

Fair: Be just and take a Nonjudgmental Stance with yourself and others. Avoid extremes and ground yourself in Wise Mind in interactions with others. Think of fair weather as being neither too hot nor too cold and without storms. Keep a moderate climate with others without whipping up bad weather. Use respectful words and actions with yourself and others. Others do *not* need to earn your respect. We treat others with respect because it builds our own self-worth. Respond rather than react in relationships.

Apologies Not Needed: Do not engage in unneeded apologetic behavior. Do not apologize for having an opinion or for your own viewpoints. You are allowed to disagree. Do not apologize for being you. Avoid apologies for things over which you have no control. Chronic, unnecessary apologies erode self-respect and devalue apologies that are genuinely needed. Note that "no apologies" does not apply to situations that require an apology (e.g., hurting someone).

Stick to Values: Use your priorities, goals, and values as guides and ground yourself in them. Choose behaviors and have interactions with others that build your self-respect. Identify what is important to you and stick to it. Know what values are non-negotiable, and when values conflict, work to resolve the conflict through Wise Mind. Live your life grounded in values.

Truth and Accountability: Be honest and accountable with yourself and others. Sometimes we avoid the truth because we are afraid of the consequences, but trying to deceive others destroys self-respect and often causes greater problems. Even if you have a great memory and can keep from getting tangled in a web of lies, *you* will still know the truth. Being accountable is more effective in most cases.

In addition, act in a manner that respects your true abilities and avoid feigned helplessness and excuses. Take responsibility for yourself.

VALUES APPLICATION

Core concept: Identify values to practice them with behaviors.

This is a partial list of values. You might have a value that is not on the list or notice some overlap between values. Review the list and circle your top 10 values. Use your selected values in the exercise that follows.

Acceptance	Consistency	Exploration
Achievement	Contentment	Expressiveness
Activity	Contribution	Fairness
Adaptability	Cooperation	Faith
Adventurousness	Courage	Family
Affectionateness	Courteousness	Fidelity
Altruism	Creativity	Financial independence
Ambition	Credibility	Firmness
Assertiveness	Decisiveness	Fitness
Attentiveness	Dependability	Freedom
Availability	Determination	Friendship
Awareness	Devotion	Fun
Balance	Dignity	Generosity
Belongingness	Discipline	Giving
Bravery	Discretion	Grace
Calm	Diversity	Gratitude
Capability	Drive	Happiness
Caring	Duty	Harmony
Challenge	Education	Health
Charity	Effectiveness	Honesty
Cleanliness	Empathy	Honor
Closeness	Encouragement	Hopefulness
Comfort	Endurance	Humility
Commitment	Energy	Humor
Compassion	Enjoyment	Hygiene
Confidence	Enthusiasm	Imagination
Connection	Excellence	Independence

Integrity	Playfulness	Service
Intelligence	Pleasantness	Sharing
Intensity	Pleasure	Simplicity
Intimacy	Popularity	Sincerity
Joy	Practicality	Spirituality
Kindness	Pragmatism	Spontaneity
Knowledge	Privacy	Stability
Leadership	Professionalism	Strength
Learning	Prosperity	Structure
Love	Relaxation	Success
Loyalty	Reliability	Support
Mindfulness	Religion	Teamwork
Modesty	Resilience	Thankfulness
Motivation	Resoluteness	Thoughtfulness
Neatness	Respect	Trust
Openness	Restraint	Truth
Optimism	Sacrifice	Usefulness
Order	Security	Warmth
Passion	Self-control	Willingness
Peace	Self-reliance	Wisdom
Persistence	Sensitivity	

Once your values are identified, you can describe specific behaviors that you can practice to live your values with intention. The following are examples for how you can complete this exercise:

I value: TRUTH

Describe three specific ways you can live this value:

1. Fill out my Diary Card more accurately
2. Tell important others when I make a mistake
3. Stop hiding liquor bottles in the garage

I value: FRIENDSHIP

Describe three specific ways you can live this value:

1. Return phone calls from my friends
2. Respect Tammy's boundaries
3. Practice GIVE skills in group

I value: PEACE

Describe three specific ways you can live this value:

1. Not yell at my wife and kids when I am angry
2. Practice MINDFULNESS exercises in the morning and at bedtime
3. Use RADICAL ACCEPTANCE to stop beating myself up for mistakes

I value: GIVING

Describe three specific ways you can live this value:

1. Give my group feedback on what they are doing well
2. Donate possessions that I have not used for a year
3. Be present in my relationships

Now it's your turn:

I value:

Describe three specific ways you can live this value:

1.

2.

3.

I value:

Describe three specific ways you can live this value:

1.

2.

3.

I value:

Describe three specific ways you can live this value:

1.

2.

3.

I value:

Describe three specific ways you can live this value:

1.

2.

3.

I value:

Describe three specific ways you can live this value:

1.

2.

3.

I value:

Describe three specific ways you can live this value:

1.
2.
3.

I value:

Describe three specific ways you can live this value:

1.
2.
3.

I value:

Describe three specific ways you can live this value:

1.
2.
3.

I value:

Describe three specific ways you can live this value:

1.
2.
3.

VALUES CONFLICT APPLICATION

Core concept: Use Wise Mind to resolve value conflicts.

Most of us know the phrase "He has his priorities mixed up." It implies that a person's values are in conflict and that an ineffective course of action has been taken. In other words, the person is making choices without considering important priorities, goals, and values.

We frequently have these conflicts. When they happen, we try to decide what will best meet the demands of the situation while still maintaining our self-respect. Use the following exercise to help you resolve value conflicts.

Describe the situation nonjudgmentally:

Describe the priorities, goals, and values in conflict:

Rank the priorities, goals, and values from most to least important:

Describe options that either follow your top-ranked value(s) or that show adequate respect across values:

Evaluate the options. (See Pros and Cons and SOLVED) Describe a course of action from Wise Mind that maintains or builds self-respect:

Note: Occasionally we must make choices that sacrifice important values. Make these decisions from Wise Mind and only when the outcome is essential.

Using GIVE (G)

Core concept: Focus on others to build and maintain relationships.

GIVE skills focus on others. We build and maintain relationships by balancing our own wants, needs, and desires with those of the people around us. Everyone benefits from healthier relationships grounded in genuine interest and validation. GIVE is also key to resolving conflicts.

Use the acronym *GIVE* to remember the building blocks (**G**enuine, **I**nterested, **V**alidate, **E**asy Manner) of this skill. These building blocks are described in further detail in the paragraphs that follow.

Genuine: Be honest, sincere, and real with others. Speak and act from your heart with caring and use mindfulness to be with others in the moment. Let others know that you value them and treat them with respect.

Interested: Interest comes from efforts to connect with a person. Let others have the focus. Listen intently to others and pause to make space before responding. Ask questions and listen to the answers.

Be mindful of your nonverbal communication. Our nonverbals communicate a great deal of information to others, both intentionally and unintentionally. Send the nonverbal messages that you want to send to others. Nonverbally, interest is communicated by looking at the person, making appropriate eye contact, and keeping your mannerisms and posture open and relaxed.

Validate: To validate means to nonjudgmentally acknowledge others' feelings, thoughts, beliefs, and experience. Validation is "walking a mile in others' shoes," and seeing life from their perspective. We validate when we find others' truth and how their experiences make sense given their life circumstances and the situation. (See VALIDATE) Remember to validate *yourself,* too.

Easy Manner: Remember the idiom "You catch more flies with honey than with vinegar." Having an easy manner means treating others with kindness and a relaxed attitude. It also means not being heavy handed with our judgments, opinions, and viewpoints. Allow space for others.

We can always raise our Interpersonal Intensity if necessary. It is often more effective to start out in a relatively relaxed and laid-back manner.

Listening (L)

Core concept: Listen to demonstrate that you care.

Listening is a skill that requires Mindfulness and practice. To listen well, we must let go of distractions and focus our attention on what is being said in the moment. Notice distractions and go back to listening one-mindfully in the moment.

We also practice Nonjudgmental Stance to listen accurately. When we Observe ourselves being defensive or planning what to say in response, we have probably lost some of the accuracy of our listening. Go back to listening one-mindfully and attend to what others are saying.

Many of us have an unconscious resistance to listening. When others say, "Listen to me," there is often an implied "Agree with me" or "Follow my directions." These unconscious assumptions can get in the way. Remember that listening does not have to mean agreement or compliance.

Reflective listening is an effective way to practice listening and to validate. With reflective listening, we mirror (or reflect) back what the other person said, either exactly or by paraphrasing the central themes. Our reflective responses can be brief. The goal is to stay attentive in the conversation and make sure we heard others, sometimes listening to what is "behind" the words.

Reflective listening is a skill that can feel awkward at first. Practice reflective listening in role-plays and in conversations. When using this skill, resist the urge to respond with your own material and instead keep the focus on others through reflection. With time and practice, you will notice that effective listening creates positive changes in relationships and maybe a decrease in conflicts.

Using VALIDATION (V)

Core concept: Use validation to connect to others.

Validation is a complicated skill. Use this expanded teaching to learn a more advanced approach to this GIVE building block.

Use the acronym *VALIDATE* to remember the building blocks (**V**alue Others, **A**sk Questions, **L**isten and Reflect, **I**dentify with Others, **D**iscuss Emotions, **A**ttend to Nonverbals, **T**urn the Mind, **E**ncourage Participation) of this skill. These building blocks are described in further detail in the paragraphs that follow.

Value Others: Seeking the inherent value in others is essential to validation. Adopt an attitude of acceptance toward others. Demonstrate your caring and concern, and let others know they are important to you.

Ask Questions: We ask questions to help clarify others' experience. Ask specific questions about what others are feeling. Ask about thoughts and beliefs. Be genuinely curious about what is behind behaviors. Use questions to draw out others' experience.

Listen and Reflect: Listen to others' answers to your questions and reflect back the major themes. Invite others to confirm your understanding (or lack of understanding). Continue to question, listen, and reflect for clarity.

Identify with Others: Work to see the world through the eyes of others. How do relationships and the world make sense to *them*? Seek to understand others, identifying when you can and accepting differences when you cannot.

Discuss Emotions: Talk about others' feelings and how they affect them from *their* perspective (not how it affects you). Acknowledging the impact of others' experience on them demonstrates understanding.

Attend to Nonverbals: Notice others' nonverbal communication to give you information about their experience. Do they look open or closed? Are they making eye contact? Read facial expressions and body language to identify feelings, and then check out your observations with others for accuracy.

Turn the Mind: Validation does not mean that we agree with others. Validation means that we nonjudgmentally accept what they feel, think, and experience and how behaviors make sense given their context. Turn the mind toward validation, especially when it is difficult to relate. Turning the mind is especially important in conflicts.

Encourage Participation: Validation can be a difficult process at times, so we need to encourage ourselves and others to be engaged with each other. Do not give up, even when understanding is hard, when you feel disconnected, or when you are in conflict with others.

What VALIDATION Is Not

Core concept: These interactions can be confused with VALIDATION.

VALIDATION is complex and takes practice. Another way to improve this skill is to understand interactions that are not experienced as VALIDATION. The following ways of relating with others often get confused with VALIDATION. Some of these ways of relating can work, but we want to minimize their use or use them in balance with true VALIDATION.

Personalizing others' experience is not validating. Keep the focus on the other person. One or maybe two self-statements that communicate your similar experience can be validating, but when we start to tell our own story, the focus leaves the other person.

VALIDATION is about connection with others' experience but not getting absorbed into it. We can validate without taking on others' distress. (See BOUNDARIES) Be with others in distress without being their distress. Also avoid taking on someone as a "project." We can show concern and connection without being responsible for the lives of others.

VALIDATION is not "fixing," offering solutions, or giving advice. These strategies are effective in some situations, but they are on the opposite end of the dialectic from VALIDATION. Most of us do not need our situations to be fixed, or we already know how to do it ourselves. Instead, we are looking for acknowledgement and understanding.

Similarly, cheerleading and encouragement are not VALIDATION. These approaches can be effective in balance with VALIDATION, but they can feel dismissive or condescending if a person has not been validated first.

It is also useful to avoid looking on the bright side, stating that it could have been worse, or one-upping others to try to put their issues into perspective (or accomplish something else). These approaches do not usually work well. Even if what the other person is saying does not seem like a big deal to you, remember that it may be a big deal to him or her.

Last, know that VALIDATION is not agreeing or giving in. You can validate others' experience even if you disagree, are in conflict, or want some change to happen.

Using DEAR MAN (DM)

Core concept: DEAR MAN is used to get wants and needs met.

The DEAR MAN skill focuses on us. We use DEAR MAN to get our wants and needs met, to say no, and to set boundaries. This skill is the DBT version of assertiveness.

The building blocks of DEAR MAN (described later in this section) work best together, but some of them can be used independently (e.g., you can Assert without using any other DEAR MAN building blocks). Use as much or as little of DEAR MAN as is required by the situation. To be most effective, approach DEAR MAN with the following core assumptions and guidelines:

Others Cannot Read Your Mind: This includes your closest friends and family. Assume that others are oblivious to you and that they cannot tell how you are feeling or know what you want or need; it may feel personal but it is simply reality. We often get frustrated when our wants and needs go unmet and blame others. We need to *ask* for our wants and needs, say *no* when appropriate, and *maintain* our own boundaries.

Effective Communication of Your Wants and Needs Requires Words: Do not sigh, sulk, cop an attitude, get destructive, withdraw, or otherwise communicate without thoughtful words *and* expect it to work effectively. It is true that our behaviors communicate volumes, just not clearly.

DEAR MAN does not always work, even when done effectively: DEAR MAN increases the probability that you will get your wants and needs met, but it does not guarantee it.

You must be mindful of your DEAR MAN goals before you begin: Decide what is important and what is negotiable before you use DEAR MAN.

Remember to balance DEAR MAN with GIVE grounded in FAST: Attending to others (GIVE) makes them more willing to assist, accept it when you say no, and respect your boundaries. Keep track of priorities, goals, and values in relationships (FAST).

Use the acronym *DEAR MAN* to remember the building blocks (**D**escribe, **E**xpress, **A**ssert, **R**eward, **M**indful, **A**ppear Confident, **N**egotiate) of this skill. These building blocks are described in further detail in the paragraphs that follow.

Describe: Use Observe and Describe to outline the situation in nonjudgmental language. Identify the facts that will support your request, your reason for saying no, or your need for a boundary.

Express: Share your opinions and feelings if they relate and will help others to understand the situation. Sometimes you may choose not to include this step.

Assert: Ask clearly for what you want or need, say no, or set your boundary. Establish your DEAR MAN goals up front so you know what you want out of the situation and work to be straightforward and matter of fact. The Assert step is essential. Otherwise, no one will know what you want or need.

Reward: Let others know what is in it for them. How will meeting your wants and needs, accepting your refusal, or respecting your boundaries benefit the relationship? Try to focus on rewards rather than threats. Create opportunities for others to feel positive about their help or respect for you. However, sometimes we need to discuss consequences instead of rewards. Again, be matter of fact. Avoid ultimatums that will box everyone in.

Mindful: Use a "broken record" approach. Others will often try to change the subject or throw in comments to derail you. Repeat your request or limits over and over again. (Notice how children do this effectively with their parents.) Also be aware of when the broken record technique is not working and switch strategies accordingly.

Appear Confident: Act as if you feel confident even if you do not. Pretend you have the confidence you have seen someone else model. Use an assertive tone of voice, make eye contact, and use confident body language. Be mindful of your facial expression (keeping it relatively neutral) as well as your posture and overall personal appearance. Use nonverbal communication to your advantage. Write down and practice your DEAR MAN skills before using them so you feel more confident in the actual situation.

Negotiate: Negotiation means that we strike compromises and are willing to give to get. Decide what compromises make sense if you cannot meet your desired DEAR MAN goal(s). If you get stuck, turn the issue over to the other person for options to solve it; for example, say, "What do you think will work?"

Turning the tables shifts the dialectical balance and can get the process moving again.

Negotiation is a dialectical strategy to get wants and needs met by meeting someplace in the middle. In some cases, you may decide in Wise Mind that negotiation is not an option.

DEAR MAN Factors to Consider

Core concept: Consider factors that can increase your effectiveness with using DEAR MAN.

Be in WISE MIND: Wise Mind is essential for the effective use of DEAR MAN. If you are not in Wise Mind, consider soothing your emotions before using DEAR MAN in most cases. (Sometimes using DEAR MAN based in emotion mind is needed, e.g., if safety is an immediate issue.)

Use GIVE First: Start an interaction with GIVE to increase your effectiveness. Others are more receptive when you consider their feelings, point of view, and situation. GIVE can open doors for using DEAR MAN.

Think About Timing: It's been said that "timing is everything." They also say, "There's no time like the present." Both of these sayings have truth. Consider whether the timing of your use of DEAR MAN seems to favor it, but do not use timing as an excuse to put off using DEAR MAN when you need to, especially if the situation is time sensitive.

Direct DEAR MAN Appropriately: Make sure you speak to someone who can actually respond to your use of DEAR MAN. Sometimes it is difficult to predict if someone will respond well to your use of DEAR MAN. Start where you can and be respectful at all times, then move on to a different person if your use of DEAR MAN is not working. Remember that even if one person may not be able to help you when you use DEAR MAN, he or she might have influence with the next person you address.

Do Not Give Up: DEAR MAN is a difficult skill that varies in its effectiveness. Practice it in everyday situations and you will improve your overall assertiveness.

Your DEAR MAN Bill of Rights

Core concept: We all have DEAR MAN rights that we work to exercise with responsibility.

Review the bill of rights below. Refer to it to encourage yourself to use DEAR MAN. Also, remember that rights require responsibility, so use DEAR MAN mindfully and effectively. Choose your "DEAR MAN" moments wisely.

- I have the right to be treated with respect.
- I have the right to my own opinions.
- I have the right to express my feelings.
- I have the right to stand up for my values.
- I have the right to disagree with others.
- I have the right to understand a request before agreeing.
- I have the right to ask for information.
- I have the right to take time to think about a request.
- I have the right to say no without guilt.
- I have the right to ask for my wants and needs.
- I have the right to set healthy boundaries with others.
- I have the right to be in Wise Mind before I get into a discussion.
- I have the right to disengage from a conflict.
- I have other rights related to my needs and wants.

List other DEAR MAN rights:

Conflict Resolution

Core concept: Conflict Resolution takes a balance of Interpersonal Effectiveness skills.

We all have conflicts with others (or may avoid them at all costs). Use the following steps to guide you through conflicts.

1. Address issues proactively with DEAR MAN to keep the potential for and intensity of conflicts lower.

2. When in conflict, step back and see if you and others are in Wise Mind. If you want to win or be "right" more than seeking understanding and resolution, you are probably not in Wise Mind. Emotion mind conflicts are rarely effective. If you or the other person are not in Wise Mind, disengage and discuss the issue later. Use Distress Tolerance before getting back into the issue(s).

3. Consider the relevant issues. Use Wise Mind to consider whether this is a conflict worth having right now with this person. Consider your priorities, goals, values, and the nature of the conflict. Pick your conflicts wisely.

4. Use FAST throughout any interpersonal situation and especially with conflict. Lowering yourself to another's "level" will decrease your self-respect and will rarely result in an effective outcome.

5. Start with Listening and GIVE. Think about companies with great customer service. They avoid arguing and listen instead and then let you know they understand your problem. This approach frequently defuses arguments.

6. Use Nonjudgmental Stance and you might find that you agree with at least some of what the other person has to say. Breathe and give some space before you respond. Many conflicts escalate because of a mutual lack of listening coupled with rapid-fire responses.

7. Use DEAR MAN effectively. Be clear about your wants and needs, saying no, or setting boundaries. Do so in a matter of fact way without calling names, labeling, judging, or getting into extremes.

8. Use Radical Acceptance when conflicts are not resolved or when others are upset and angry. Not all conflicts have an immediate resolution. Sometimes

we need to step away and let it be. When resolution seems unlikely or when the conflict is escalating, gently disengage yourself and agree to revisit it later.

9. Remember that negotiation and making Wise Mind concessions are useful. Stay away from all or nothing in situations and work the dialectic. (See MIDDLE Cs)

Interpersonal Intensity (II)

Core concept: Begin your use of DEAR MAN skills at an effective intensity level.

Effective use of DEAR MAN sometimes depends on our level of intensity. Assertiveness is a dialectical concept, with passivity on one end and aggressiveness on the other:

Core Concept

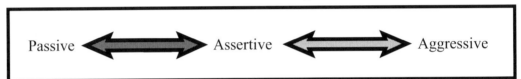

There are times to be more passive or more aggressive, but the most effective level of assertiveness is usually someplace in the middle. When we are too passive, it is easy for others to dismiss us, but when we are too aggressive, others get defensive and resist our demands. Use Observe and Describe to make a Wise Mind assessment of each unique situation.

It works well to start in the low-middle end of the dialectic in most situations. From the low-middle end, you can dial up the intensity if needed; it is less effective to start out too intense and then try to dial it down.

Consider your baseline interpersonal style when applying Interpersonal Intensity. If you are normally passive, an effective DEAR MAN level will probably feel uncomfortably aggressive. If you are normally aggressive, an effective DEAR MAN level will probably feel uncomfortably passive. Closely Observe others' reactions and responsiveness and adjust your Interpersonal Intensity accordingly.

DEAR MAN (DM) Application

Core concept: Use this worksheet to develop your DEAR MAN skills.

Describe what you want or need, what you need to say no to, or the boundary you need to set:

Describe (stick to facts):

Express (your opinions and feelings if needed):

Assert (be direct and specific):

Reward (what is in it for the other person?):

Describe how you can appear confident:

Describe negotiations you are willing to make:

Shifting Thoughts

Core concept: Thoughts are not right or wrong; it is more important to see if they work.

Many of us have been told that it is "all in our heads" or that there is something wrong or inaccurate with our thoughts and beliefs. These viewpoints invalidate our experience. The effect is that we learn not to trust ourselves, and we become defensive and guarded about our thoughts and beliefs. We then feel vulnerable when asked to evaluate them. That sense of vulnerability and defensive stance serve to protect us from further invalidation.

Dialectically, our thoughts and beliefs come from somewhere, and they make sense given the context of that place. Most of the time, our thoughts and beliefs have or have had adaptive functions. They may have helped us fit into our environments so we could survive and function the best that we could.

It is not about our thoughts and beliefs being right or wrong, accurate or inaccurate, but whether they "work" or are functional in a given situation.

For example, someone who grew up with critical parents may think that all other people will be critical, too. That thought or belief has worked in the past because it protected the person in a world that could be mean and punishing. However, when thoughts and beliefs become too generalized or extreme, they lose their function at times. In this example, the thought or belief will be less effective when applied to most everyone in most situations.

As an alternative, it may be useful for that person to see whether the general thought or belief about critical people works in a specific situation. A dialectical shift in the thought or belief could be more effective. Dialectical shifts lead to more flexible thoughts and beliefs about ourselves, others, situations, and the world.

The key to dialectical thinking is being in Wise Mind. Making dialectical shifts in thoughts and beliefs involves validating emotions and accessing our ability to reason. In this module, we focus on a method for shifting thoughts and beliefs as well as look at common "stuck" thoughts and their dialectical remedies.

Using REASON (RE)

Core concept: Dialectics help develop effective thoughts and beliefs.

Use the acronym *REASON* to remember the building blocks (**R**ational, **E**motions Matter, **A**lternative Views, **S**elf-Trust, **O**ld Beliefs, **N**ew Thoughts and Beliefs) of this skill. These building blocks are described in further detail in the paragraphs that follow.

Rational: Is the thought or belief rational coming from reason or Wise Mind? Does it work in the present situation? Remember that we all get stuck in thoughts and beliefs that do not work in certain situations so be nonjudgmental with yourself. Remember that our thoughts and beliefs "make sense" given the context from which they originated even if they do not work in the present situation. Check thoughts and beliefs with a trusted friend, family member, or other person.

Emotions Matter (Validate):   Remember that emotions are important, as is the information they provide. Sometimes emotions give us the most accurate information. Respect and validate your emotions to help you make shifts in thoughts or beliefs.

Alternative Views (Dialectic):   Develop alternative views to consider alongside the original thoughts or beliefs. Take time to evaluate how each alternative view may work in the present situation. Will a different "place" on the dialectic be more effective in the present situation? There are many ways to think about the same situation.

Self-Trust (Develop):   People who have been chronically invalidated do not trust their own thoughts and beliefs. Begin to notice times when your thoughts and beliefs work well in situations, and give yourself credit. When you learn to trust your thoughts and beliefs during these effective times, you will develop the foundation needed to recognize when shifting thoughts is needed in other situations.

Old Beliefs (Balanced With):   Respect old thoughts and belief systems. Remember that they have served purposes in different situations. The goal is not to negate old thoughts and beliefs. In time, thoughts and beliefs that are no longer useful will diminish on their own.

New Thoughts and Beliefs: New thoughts and beliefs will bring new options to how you think about yourself, others, situations, and the world. The ability to think dialectically will become part of your behavioral repertoire, and new thoughts and beliefs will contribute to a more satisfying life.

STUCK THOUGHTS AND DIALECTICAL SHIFTS APPLICATION

Core concept: Practice Dialectical Shifts with common stuck thoughts.

Certain common types of stuck thoughts benefit from Dialectical Shifts. For each one, make the concept relevant by identifying when you notice being stuck and how you can shift the thought to be more effective. Readers interested in the origins of these stuck thoughts and complete explanations of cognitive therapies can refer to the many works of pioneers Albert Ellis and Aaron T. Beck.

Black and White Thoughts (Either/or; Dichotomous; or All-or-Nothing Thinking): Words that signal this type of stuck thinking include *always*, *never, every*, and *all the time*, among others. Black and white thoughts feed emotional extremes and rarely work well. This approach to thinking leads to rigidity and inflexibility in situations and relationships.

Dialectical Shift: If your thoughts seem extreme, think of opposite thoughts or beliefs, and then start to identify middle-ground ways of thinking. You may not believe the opposite thoughts or beliefs, but the intention is to practice flexibility in your thinking.

Describe when you do this and how you can shift:

Regret Orientation (Woulda, Coulda, Shoulda Thinking; or Hindsight Bias): It is easy to look back with the information you have now and regret what you did or did not do. As they say, "hindsight is 20/20." Regret orientation keeps us stuck in the past, rather than focusing on what we can do effectively right now.

Dialectical Shift: Rather than dwelling on past mistakes, focus on what you can do to be effective in the present moment. (See Radical Acceptance or Everyday Acceptance)

Describe when you do this and how you can shift:

Mind-Reading: Many of us believe we know others' thoughts, and that belief causes us to feel or act in a certain manner. Most of us are not very good mind-readers in reality, so our feelings and actions are not based on very accurate information.

Dialectical Shift: When you catch yourself mind-reading, check out your assumptions with other people, especially the person whose mind you arc trying to read. Remember to use your DEAR MAN skills.

Describe when you do this and how you can shift:

Minimization: Minimization happens when we take something large or significant and reduce it to something that is very small. We do this to reduce the emotional impact of a situation, but the result is that we end up invalidating our emotions. We also do this when we do not want to face difficult realities.

Dialectical Shift: Observe and Describe the situation accurately without adding or subtracting. Remember to validate your feelings.

Describe when you do this and how you can shift:

Magnification: Magnification is the opposite of minimization. It happens when we take something that is small or insignificant and exaggerate it to something that is very large. It is like looking at a kitten through a magnifying glass and seeing a tiger. The result of magnification is amplifying our feelings.

Dialectical Shift: Like with minimization, Observe and Describe the situation accurately without adding or subtracting.

Describe when you do this and how you can shift:

Catastrophizing: Catastrophizing is an extreme form of magnification. It involves taking a situation and continuing to build it and build it and build it in our minds into a calamity with dire consequences.

Dialectical Shift: Focus on the *one* situation or problem at hand without exaggerating it. Remember that most situations do not end up with extreme and dire consequences. Take one thing at a time. Alternatively, purposefully catastrophize to the point of absurdity to help yourself see that your fears are not realistic.

Describe when you do this and how you can shift:

Fortune-Telling (Crystal Ball Gazing): Fortune-telling is the attempt to predict the future, usually in negative ways. It assumes that we already know what is going to happen, and it often causes emotions of anxiety and dread. Most of us are not very accurate at predicting the future in reality.

Dialectical Shift: Rather than let a negative prediction of the future paralyze you, focus on what you can do effectively right now to cope with your situation or problem. Stay in the present moment.

Describe when you do this and how you can shift:

Overgeneralization: Overgeneralization involves taking a small bit of information and applying it broadly across all kinds of different people and situations.

Dialectical Shift: Do not assume that your knowledge fits all people and all situations. Acknowledge when your information does fit, and actively look for times when it does not. Be open to not knowing all of the facts.

Describe when you do this and how you can shift:

Selective Information Gathering (Selective Abstraction; Mental Filter; or Confirmation Bias): Sometimes we only gather information that fits with our current thought or belief. This approach tends to validate our thought or belief, but it can lead to ineffective choices due to a poverty of information and viewpoints.

Dialectical Shift: Actively gather information and viewpoints that are different from your own. Remember that you do not need to agree with these different perspectives, but that they may lead you to greater flexibility and more effective choices.

Describe when you do this and how you can shift:

Labeling (Judging): Labeling is an approach that takes a person or situation and reduces it to only a name. Labels fail to look at people and situations in a more holistic manner and miss important subtleties or nuances.

Dialectical Shift: Gently let go of the need to label a person or situation. Instead, Observe and Describe nonjudgmentally. Understand that the world is more complex than labels and judging.

Describe when you do this and how you can shift:

Personalization: Personalization makes it all about you. Even when situations feel personal, they often are not. We feel the weight of the world when we take so many situations and others' issues and problems personally.

Dialectical Shift: Use a Teflon® Mind. Remember that most of the time it is not about you. Take responsibility for what is yours (if it fits Wise Mind) and gently let go of the rest.

Describe when you do this and how you can shift:

Emotion Mind "Reasoning": Emotion mind reasoning means having your thoughts and beliefs come from an emotion mind place without factoring in reason mind or Wise Mind.

Dialectical Shift: Use What and How skills to access Wise Mind. Alternatively, use Distress Tolerance skills to soothe your emotions before shifting thoughts and beliefs.

Describe when you do this and how you can shift:

Should Statements: These statements get us stuck because they focus on judgments rather than the realities of a particular situation or interaction. Reality unfolds in ways that do not fit our preferences (i.e., what "should" happen).

Dialectical Shift: Focus on "what is," not what "should be." Stop "shoulding" on yourself and others.

Describe when you do this and how you can shift:

Discounting Positives: Many times we focus on the negatives or the downside of situations and are blind to positives. Sometimes we minimize or negate positives about ourselves, others, situations, or the world. Discounting positives is undialectical.

Dialectical Shift: Seek out positives, upsides, and silver linings for balance. Own the positives about yourself and give yourself credit. Find the positives in people and situations that seem negative.

Describe when you do this and how you can shift:

Blaming: Blaming makes everyone but us responsible for our problems and difficulties. When we blame, we give up our power and control and are utterly dependent on others to fix a situation (or our lives).

Dialectical Shift: Someone or something else may be responsible for a problem, but your power and control comes from focusing on how you can influence situations and your life, if only through choosing how you respond.

Describe when you do this and how you can shift:

A Mindfulness Application to Shifting Thoughts

Core concept: Mindfulness skills can lessen the impact of negative thoughts and beliefs.

Observe and Describe thoughts and beliefs nonjudgmentally. Remove the personalization from your thoughts and beliefs by separating yourself from them. This approach is called "defusing" and is a part of Acceptance and Commitment Therapy (ACT) (Hayes et al., 1999).

In other words, Describe thoughts and beliefs in ways that are not about you. Thoughts are just thoughts and only have the power we give them. "Nobody likes me" becomes "I am having a thought that nobody likes me." "I can't do this" becomes "I am thinking that I can't do this again." "This is stupid" becomes "I am using a judgment word in this moment." "I'm so ugly" becomes "I'm thinking that I'm ugly again."

As we simply Observe and Describe, we accept rather than judge or fight thoughts and beliefs. By doing so, we remove much of their emotional power and stay unstuck.

Readers who find this approach to thoughts helpful can find additional explanations and applications in books on Acceptance and Commitment Therapy.

REASON AND SHIFTING THOUGHTS APPLICATION

Core concept: Use this worksheet to practice Shifting Thoughts.

Observe and Describe the thought or belief:

Is the thought or belief rational from reason mind or Wise Mind? Is it functional or working right now? Is it an example of a stuck thought? Describe:

Validate your current emotion (it matters too):

Describe at least two alternative viewpoints on the dialectic:

Balance these alternative viewpoints with your original thought or belief. Describe any differences in your thoughts, beliefs, or feelings:

Clinical Policies, Contingencies, and Related Forms

This section contains brief explanations of important policies and contingencies that can structure your DBT program and/or individual therapy. Commonly used client forms are also included.

The explanations are intended to get you started. The concepts are explained at more length and with some differences in Linehan's book and manual (1993a; 1993b). These source materials are recommended for those serious about DBT and can provide you with other ideas.

Use the materials in this section as they are or adapt them for your unique population and setting. These materials are simply examples and are not intended to serve everybody. Customize them as needed, because one size does not fit all.

Many of the forms included were developed by people across several programs and settings over a period of many years as services evolved. The forms were then revised again for this book. Look to your clients to inform you what will be effective and make thoughtful changes over time. All of these are "living" documents.

Remember that structure, rules, and expectations constitute important facets of all programs and individual therapy. Clients need this to thrive, and clients rise to expectations. Therapists similarly need the direction that comes from these and similar policies to keep their programs and their clients on track.

Last, note the explanation on clinical outcomes. This section is not intended to be comprehensive. It is intended to get you thinking about how you can measure and demonstrate outcomes in your setting with your clients. Explore options and commit to the collection of outcomes so you can monitor and adjust therapy. Monitoring clinical outcomes is at the heart of evidence-based practice.

Commitment Agreements

DBT can be a long-term commitment for clients. Consider stages of change (Prochaska et al., 2007) when you discuss commitment with clients and try to meet clients at their stage. Stages of change can swing rapidly based on unforeseen influences in and out of therapy. Premature judgments and ruling out clients struggling to attach to therapy can result in lost opportunities. "Perfect" candidates for therapy are the stuff of random clinical trials and not real life.

It is helpful to orient clients to the expected course of treatment required to achieve significant clinical change and improvement in functioning. Outcome data and your clinical expertise can assist in explaining the course of treatment for individual clients.

Many DBT programs require a significant time commitment of up to one year, with the opportunity to recommit to further therapy following the initial contract. A long-term commitment is helpful, but many clients have reservations about investing in something new and uncertain for the long haul. (Can you blame them?)

A middle-ground option is a good faith commitment to try the DBT program or individual therapy for a length of time or a number of sessions that will provide a realistic evaluation from both sides. That level of commitment may vary by client and is based on the expected time required to connect and experience benefits; if applicable, try to balance this commitment with the expectations and structure of your program. The important piece is that you and the client agree on a timeline, expectations, and how the mutual investment will be evaluated.

Commitment agreements, whether standard to your program or individualized, need to be discussed up front and preferably put in writing. Remember that commitment has to do with length of time or number of sessions, but *not* with changing program or individual rules and expectations or with taking an "à la carte" approach to an otherwise comprehensive program.

COMMITMENT AGREEMENT FORM

The following information has been explained to me, with an opportunity to ask questions for clarification:

- My diagnosis
- My expected course of treatment
- My individualized treatment plan with initial goals
- The program and/or individual rules and expectations
- The program and/or individual attendance policy
- The cost and my financial responsibility (e.g., copays, deductibles, payment agreements)
- Other important information

I agree to make a good faith investment in the program and/or individual therapy with my willing participation for a period of _____ or _____ sessions. As a part of this commitment, I agree to follow the program and/or individual rules, expectations, and attendance policy. At the conclusion of this commitment period, my therapist(s) and I will evaluate the course of treatment and decide among the following options:

- Continue the program and/or individual therapy with a new commitment agreement
- Make an appropriate referral
- Other arrangements

Signed by client: _____ Date: _____

Signed by therapist: _____ Date: _____

Original to client; copy to chart

Program and Individual Therapy Rules and Expectations

DBT programs and individual therapy require rules and expectations. Rules and expectations keep clients safe and help them know what is expected. Think about times when you have been in unclear situations (e.g., when you had a laissez-faire boss or a teacher without a grading system or syllabus) and how uncomfortable, anxiety provoking, or frustrating those times were.

Clients who have dysregulated emotions and chaotic behaviors need structure and containment to learn new skills and thrive. Not being clear about what is expected is unfair and puts clients in unneeded distress.

Sometimes we have clients who resist rules, expectations, and structure, and our approach can cause behavioral outbursts that buck the system. These reactions can tempt us to abandon ship and allow for greater flexibility and a lack of accountability.

As a rule, if you abandon your structure or change your rules (programmatically or individually) for a client, you are participating in Therapy-Interfering Behavior (TIB) with the client. Clients do not always need to agree to rules and expectations, but they need to respect them. Sticking to rules and expectations is difficult for both clients and therapists, but it models what happens in real life. If you have difficulties holding clients accountable, then seek consultation.

It is compassionate to have rules and expectations and to stick to them, even if the consequence is discharging a client from the program. Be clear and consistent; say what you do and do what you say. To do otherwise recreates the type of environment that may have created the client's problems in the first place.

Rules and expectations need to be discussed and acknowledged up front. Clients need to know the rules and expectations to be accountable to them. Consider the use of a Behavior Contract (see later) for clients who require additional accountability.

When presenting rules and expectations, have clients tell you the rationale for each one instead of explaining it to them. This type of presentation lets clients "own" the rules and expectations. Be sure to clearly post rules and expectations in program areas.

DBT Program Expectations

- Members are expected to attend all scheduled sessions. All absences must be planned with therapists prior to the absence by phone or in person. Documentation of absences may be requested. Three consecutive absences without approval will be grounds for discharge.
- Members are accountable to the attendance policies and may be discharged for violation of these policies.
- Members are to maintain confidentiality. Group issues are not to be discussed outside of group or during break. Breaking confidentiality may be grounds for discharge.
- Members are expected to participate in skills teaching, to complete assignments, to present Diary Cards, and to give validation, support, and suggestions to peers.
- Members are expected to take time to problem solve and practice skills whenever significant distress is reported.
- Members are expected to complete homework and change analyses as assigned.
- Members are not to engage in SI/SIB/TIB behaviors when on premises. These behaviors on premises will be grounds for immediate discharge.
- Members are not to come to group under the influence of drugs or alcohol.
- Members' feedback and behavior is expected to be respectful at all times. Anyone giving disrespectful feedback or engaging in disrespectful behavior may be asked to leave.
- Members are encouraged to form friendships with others in group. However, members are expected to be clear about their personal boundaries and be respectful of others' personal boundaries.
- Romantic or intimate relationships are not allowed between group members.
- Friendships with others in group may not be private and must remain skillful.
- Members are not allowed to use alcohol, drugs, or engage in unskillful behaviors together.
- Members are not allowed to keep secrets regarding other group members' harmful behaviors.
- Members are encouraged to use other members for support outside of group. However, members are not obligated to be available to others outside of group. Again, members are expected to be clear about their boundaries and respectful of others' boundaries.
- Members may not call other members after they have been engaged in SI/SIB/TIB.
- Members are expected to attend all scheduled professional appointments and comply with prescribed medications.
- Members are expected to honor payment agreements for copays, deductibles, and uncovered services.
- Violation of group rules may result in consequences including homework, behavior change analysis, suspension, and/or discharge.

DBT Individual Expectations

- Clients must attend all scheduled sessions. Cancelled or missed sessions will be treated as therapy-interfering behavior (TIB) unless negotiated up front and cleared by the therapist.
- Clients in the DBT program who miss sessions will be accountable to the attendance policy of the program (i.e., 90% attendance of all DBT sessions).
- Clients not in the DBT program will be accountable for attending 90% (9 out of 10) of all scheduled individual sessions. Two no-shows (not coming to session and not calling ahead to cancel) to individual therapy will result in discharge.
- Clients are expected to be on time for sessions.
- Clients are expected to complete homework and change analysis as assigned.
- Clients are expected to participate in safety assessments and safety planning. Being unable to commit to safety or being unwilling to engage in safety commitments and planning will result in hospitalization.
- Clients are expected to honor payment agreements for copays, deductibles, and uncovered services.
- Clients are expected to follow other rules and policies.

Attendance Policy and Contracts

DBT program and individual therapists need to be clear about attendance policies for clients. A clear and up-front policy is an important way to instill expectations and to avoid becoming a crisis drop-in center.

Attendance is required in school, college, work, and relationships, making it a primary life skill. Have your clients practice this life skill by expecting their presence at all program (and other) appointments.

The attendance policies and contracts that follow are examples of how attendance expectations can be addressed. The intention of attendance contracts is to keep clients engaged in the DBT program and/or individual therapy. Therapists need to decide what type of attendance policy and contracts work for their unique populations and settings and design their own if needed. The specific policy is less important than the fact that it is clear what the policy entails, how clients are expected to be accountable, and most importantly, how the policy will be enforced. Remember that being consistent is one way to respect clients.

Along with attendance, also expect clients to be on time (and be on time yourself). Lateness by the client (or you) is TIB and needs to be addressed as such. If a client has a pattern of being significantly late (e.g., 15 minutes), consider counting future lateness toward the attendance policy. (Let the client know this up front.)

DBT Program Attendance Policy

Consistent attendance of your DBT program is essential for it to be effective for you and other program members. Attendance, timeliness, and consistency are also important life skills.

It is expected that program members attend appointments at or above 90% of all scheduled sessions (individual and group). Please schedule other appointments around your DBT program.

If you fall below 90% attendance, you will be put on an attendance contract, and your treatment team will be contacted. The contract is for 10 sessions; you must attend 9 out of 10 of these sessions to complete and go off of the attendance contract. If you miss more than 1 of these 10 sessions, you will be put on a discharge contract, and your team will be contacted again.

The discharge contract is also for 10 sessions. Like the attendance contract, you must attend 9 out of 10 of these sessions to complete and go off of the discharge contract. If you miss more than 1 of these 10 sessions, you will be discharged from the program and **cannot reapply for 3 months.**

Excused absences are at the discretion of your therapist(s) and may or may not be negotiable. Documentation may be required.

You are responsible for keeping your therapist(s) informed if you have to miss a session. Always call before the session if you will be absent. An absence without a call before the session will most likely not be excused.

Three consecutive no-shows (not coming and not calling ahead to cancel) to the program may result in discharge.

A leave of absence (LOA) may be granted in some cases at the discretion of the therapist(s) and/or the treatment team. LOAs must be planned with a clear time limit. It is your responsibility to keep your therapist(s) and team informed during an LOA. Documentation of an LOA may be required.

Signed by client: _____ Date: _____

Original to client; copy to file

ATTENDANCE CONTRACT

My attendance to scheduled DBT sessions has dropped below 90%.

I am on this attendance contract to get my required attendance to 90% or above of scheduled sessions.

I must attend 9 out of the next 10 scheduled sessions to complete this contract.

If I miss more than 1 of the next 10 sessions, I will move to a discharge contract.

All absences on this contract will be considered unexcused unless negotiated with my therapist BEFORE the absence. Excused absences will be granted only in extreme circumstances as approved by my therapist.

Signed by client: _____ Date: _____

Signed by therapist: _____ Date: _____

Original to client; copy to file

DISCHARGE CONTRACT

My attendance to scheduled DBT sessions has dropped below 90%, AND I have not completed the assigned ATTENDANCE CONTRACT.

I am on this discharge contract to get my required attendance to 90% or above of scheduled sessions.

I must attend 9 of the next 10 scheduled sessions to complete this contract.

If I miss more than 1 of the next 10 sessions, I will be discharged and given referrals to other treatment options.

All absences on this contract will be considered unexcused unless negotiated with my therapist BEFORE the absence. Excused absences will be granted only in extreme circumstances as approved by my therapist.

Signed by client: _____ Date: _____

Signed by therapist: _____ Date: _____

Original to client; copy to chart

Diary Cards

Diary Cards are used to track clients' symptoms, safety issues, Therapy-Interfering Behavior (TIB), and skills. Additionally, clients can track feelings, gratefulness, and virtually any other information relevant to therapy. Diary Cards can be customized to unique populations and programs with input from clients on what is important to track.

Diary Cards must be filled out mindfully on a daily basis. Give clients clear directions for how to complete Diary Cards. Clients should expect to spend 5 to 15 minutes a day to thoughtfully complete them. If a client fails to fill out a Diary Card, does it at the last minute, or otherwise completes it without thoughtful intention, treat it as TIB.

Use the Diary Card in sessions to identify treatment targets. Suicidality is the top treatment target, followed by Self-Injurious Behavior (SIB), and then TIB.

Accurate and thoughtful Diary Cards provide a wealth of information for therapists to quickly evaluate priorities for the session. Remember to use the Diary Card to validate emotions, reinforce efforts and effective skill use, and Observe and Describe patterns over time. Diary Cards are as relevant as we make them, so avoid making them a rote exercise for clients.

Diary Cards also serve to add further structure for clients in sessions and in life, keeping them grounded in skills and the therapy.

DIARY CARD EXPECTATIONS

Diary Cards help us to track both symptoms and skills. Over time, we gain greater awareness and can see the progress that comes with skill use. Diary Cards also help to identify treatment targets. Please follow these expectations when completing your Diary Card:

- Everyone fills out a Diary Card daily. Diary Cards are filled out mindfully before sessions.
- Incomplete or last-minute attempts to fill out a Diary Card will be treated as Therapy-Interfering Behavior (TIB).
- You will report honestly on your Diary Card. If there is a question of your honesty and the therapist cannot accurately assess you for safety, further assessment will happen at the hospital.
- Anytime you indicate a "yes" for Suicidal Ideation (SI), Self-Injurious Behavior (SIB), or TIB, you will take time to address any or all of those issues before any other problems. Safety planning, if applicable, will be done in the time allotted, or further assessment will happen at the hospital.
- If there is not a clear commitment to safety with a willingness to use your safety plan, you will be hospitalized.
- Anytime you have indicated a "yes" for SI, SIB, or TIB, you will be assigned a Change Analysis to do before the following session. If a clear effort has been put into its completion, you can ask your therapist or the group to assist you further. If a clear effort has not been put into its completion or if it is incomplete, you will be asked to complete it during break and may be assigned an additional Change Analysis for TIB.

DIARY CARD INSTRUCTIONS

Core concept: The Diary Card develops awareness and accountability to help you build a satisfying life.

Follow these directions:

- Fill out your Diary Card *every* day. Do it thoughtfully and bring it to all sessions.
- For the Medications (RX) section, write the number of medications you took over the number you were prescribed to take (e.g., if you took three pills and were prescribed three, you would write "3/3"). If you took all of your medications, you can write in "all" as an alternative.
- For the Depression (DEP), Anxiety (ANX), and Anger (ANG) sections, use a scale of 10 to 0 and rate the *range* of your feelings by noting the highest and lowest levels (e.g., 8–4 for ANX).
- For the Suicidal Ideation (SI), Self-Injurious Behavior (SIB), and Therapy-Interfering Behavior (TIB) sections, use a scale of 10 to 0 and rate the *range* of your urges by noting the highest and lowest levels. Additionally, use a Y (yes) or N (no) to note if you *acted* on SI, SIB, or TIB urges (e.g., 9–2/N for SIB urges).
- For the Sleep section, note the total number of hours of sleep. Make a slash mark (/) through the number if the sleep was not restful or was broken.
- For the Energy section, use a scale of 10 to 0 and rate the *range* of your energy level (e.g., 6–4).
- For the Build Mastery (BM), PLEASED (PL), and Attend to Relationships (A2R) sections use a Y (yes) or N (no). Use Y for *any* efforts to practice these skills.
- For the Other section, track any other symptom, behavior, or issue important to your treatment.
- List the skills you used to address each specific category on the Diary Card (e.g., for DEP, someone might list PL, O2E, and DM).
- On the back side of the Diary Card, write in your feelings, positive events, and things for which you are grateful each day.

Diary Card

	RX	DEP	ANX	ANG	SI	SIB	TIB	Sleep	Energy	BM	PL	A2R	Other
MON													
Skills													
TUE													
Skills													
WED													
Skills													
THU													
Skills													
FRI													
Skills													
SAT													
Skills													
SUN													
Skills													

FEELINGS	POSITIVE EVENTS	GRATEFULNESS
FEELINGS	POSITIVE EVENTS	GRATEFULNESS
FEELINGS	POSITIVE EVENTS	GRATEFULNESS
FEELINGS	POSITIVE EVENTS	GRATEFULNESS
FEELINGS	POSITIVE EVENTS	GRATEFULNESS
FEELINGS	POSITIVE EVENTS	GRATEFULNESS
FEELINGS	POSITIVE EVENTS	GRATEFULNESS

Safety Plans and Contracts

Identify clients with a history of Suicidal Ideation (SI) and/or Self-Injurious Behavior (SIB) at the initial intake assessment. All of these clients need a Safety Plan that is proactively created.

Most clients already have "safety skills," but they may not be able to label or name them. The lack of a name for such skills, along with the lack of a plan, makes it difficult for clients to use these skills consistently and effectively. Careful questioning will reveal clients' ways of staying safe and other strengths and resources to build on.

Check safety early in each session and dedicate some time to review and build on the safety plan. Rehearse safety contingencies in sessions (e.g., what skills would you use if your spouse storms out? What if no one is home and you're scared? What skills can you use?).

Make sure clients practice the skills in their plan so they develop the competency to use them in crisis. As clients build skills, have them further expand their safety plan. A safety plan is a "living" document, both metaphorically and literally.

Mindfully and consistently reinforce safety behaviors (clients are typically "safe" more than "unsafe") and create safety homework for crisis behaviors and unhealthy coping. The requirement of a Change Analysis and active work on the safety plan is a response cost and is also needed for clients to reach their goals.

Remember that safety is one of the few either/or issues in treatment, with clear "yes" and "no" answers required to questions about safety. An unclear safety commitment and/or lack of willingness to use the safety plan indicates that hospitalization is needed. Clients have the sole responsibility for their safety.

See the following examples of safety expectations, plans, and contracts. Like most forms in this book, adapt them as needed for your clients.

SAFETY EXPECTATIONS

Safety will be assessed each session. Identify ALL safety concerns on your Diary Card. Clients with a history of safety issues will also be asked about safety and reinforced for effective safety behaviors.

Please refer to the following safety expectations:

- All clients will accurately report safety issues on the Diary Card.
- All clients with current or a history of safety issues will develop a Safety Plan. The Safety Plan will be practiced, updated, and reviewed regularly.
- Clients will willingly participate in safety assessments in the time allotted. Clients unwilling to cooperate will be hospitalized.
- All safety assessments and safety planning must be completed in the allotted time and by the end of the session. Clients without a safety commitment by the end of the session will be hospitalized.
- All clients with safety issues will be asked to commit to safety. A safety commitment is a "yes" or "no" regarding willingness to use the Safety Plan. Clients without a clear commitment to safety who are suicidal will be hospitalized.
- Clients hospitalized will be sent ONLY by ambulance or police.
- Clients hospitalized will be sent with a Change Analysis to work on and a Safety Plan to update. These assignments will be completed during the hospital stay and/or before returning to the program/individual therapy.

Signed by client: _____ Date: _____

Original to client; copy to chart

SAFETY CONTRACT AND PLAN

I, _____, contract for my safety. This means that I will not act on my plan to commit suicide. I will use the skills listed below to assist with my safety and call the people in my support system as needed. I will call 911 or admit myself into the hospital if unsafe and BEFORE acting on urges.

DBT skills I will use to maintain my safety:

1.
2.
3.
4.
5.
6.
7.

Team members/other people in my support system/crisis numbers I can call for help BEFORE ACTING ON URGES:

1.   Phone number:
2.   Phone number:
3.   Phone number:
4. Crisis Resource(s):   Phone number(s):
5. Emergency   911

Signed by client: _____   Date: _____

Signed by therapist: _____   Date: _____

Original to client; copy to chart

185

CRISIS SAFETY PLAN

Name:

Crisis Behavior:

Warning Signs and Triggers:

Specific Plan to Maintain Safety until Next Session (list specific skills/behaviors under each section):

Mindfulness Skills:

Interpersonal Skills:

Emotion Regulation Skills:

Distress Tolerance Skills:

Skills from Other Modules:

Diagnoses and Symptoms:

Medications:

1.   Dosage

2.   Dosage

3.   Dosage

4.   Dosage

5.   Dosage

6.   Dosage

Medical Alerts (Allergies, etc.):

Contacts (People to Call for Support):

      Therapist: Phone number:

      Psychiatrist: Phone number:

      Case Manager: Phone number:

      Family: Phone number:

      Friends: Phone number:

      Other: Phone number:

If you have a plan and intent to act on your urges, call 911 or go to your nearest emergency room.

SAFETY CONTRACT

I, _____, contract for my safety. This means I will not act on any plan to commit suicide. I will use my skills to assist with my safety, call my team members, crisis resources, and/or people in my support system BEFORE ACTING ON URGES. I will call 911 and/or admit myself into the hospital if needed.

As a part of my safety contract, I will also attend all scheduled appointments and my DBT program.

Not attending group or other appointments as planned will be considered a violation of my willingness to commit to safety and will be treated as Therapy- Interfering Behavior (TIB).

Signed by client: _____ Date: _____

Signed by therapist: _____ Date: _____

Original to client; copy to chart

Behavior Change (Chain) Analysis

Behavior analysis is an integral part of DBT. Do not be intimidated by behavior analysis. At its core, behavior analysis is simply establishing a sequence of what came before and what came after any action or behavior you want to better understand (e.g., a target behavior like SI or a TIB, the use of a skill or effective behavior, etc.).

Behavior analysis increases awareness and connections so clients can comprehend the context of their behaviors. Understanding the context allows clients to be validated, and then they can explore the possibility of alternative choices (skills) at each step of the sequence. Establishing the sequential "chain" with alternatives empowers clients to change. See the written and visual change analysis examples to understand this process in action.

Sometimes clients perceive behavior analysis to be a punishment. While this perception can decrease target behaviors for certain clients, it may be more beneficial to frame behavior analysis as a learning tool for change (thus, the phrase *"change" analysis* rather than *"chain" analysis*). We want clients to be curious about the context from which behaviors arise and not "punished" for having those behaviors in the first place. Framing behavior analysis as a tool for understanding and change better fits with DBT philosophies.

Behavior analysis can also be used to understand how effective behaviors and skills occurred. Clients frequently see these effective moments as chance occurrences, and behavior analysis can consolidate gains for them by relating these behaviors to a larger context. Using behavior analysis to examine effective behaviors further strengthens the approach as a learning tool.

Integrate behavior analysis into your therapy approach and give clients blank forms to practice behavior analysis between therapy sessions. When clients learn and practice this process, it becomes a powerful agent of change.

VISUAL BEHAVIOR CHANGE ANALYSIS DIRECTIONS

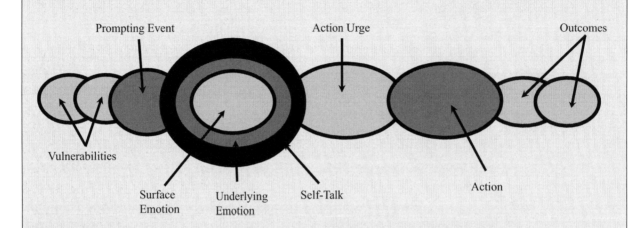

DIRECTIONS: *The more you understand about behaviors you want to change, the more you can be effective in the use of your skills to meet that goal! Start anywhere on the change (chain) analysis and work forward and/or backward to figure out each link, then identify other skills or choices you could make with your new awareness. Remember to be NONJUDGMENTAL with yourself, the situation, and others. The following explains each identified link, but remember that you can add as many links as you need to understand your process and that EVERY LINK PRESENTS AN OPPORTUNITY FOR CHANGE! Also, look for skills that you might have already been using but had not noticed or for which you need more practice. Chances are you have been using skills!*

Vulnerabilities: What made you vulnerable to the prompting event (and what unfolded after it)? Examples might include not doing self-care, having a tough day, getting into a conflict, or other stressors. Be as specific as possible.

Prompting Event: What happened? Describe in nonjudgmental, descriptive words.

Surface Emotion: What feeling(s) occurred after the prompting event that was/were most easily noticed?

Underlying Emotion: Was there a feeling or feelings further below the surface? Examples might include feeling hurt or embarrassed under anger or feeling guilty under depression.

Self-Talk: What automatic thoughts or beliefs were happening that fed your emotions and the following action urge?

Action Urge: What did the feelings pull you to do? This link is a critical moment of choice in changing a behavior.

Action: This is the behavior you might want to change. However, remember that using skills at earlier links might effectively change your action/behavior.

Outcomes: What happened after the behavior you want to change? What did you gain and/or lose, in both the short term and the long term? Did the outcomes cause a new vulnerability or stressor and/or cycle back to the beginning again?

SOLUTIONS: At each step, brainstorm skills or choices that could create behavior change and more effective outcomes.

VISUAL BEHAVIOR CHANGE ANALYSIS FORM

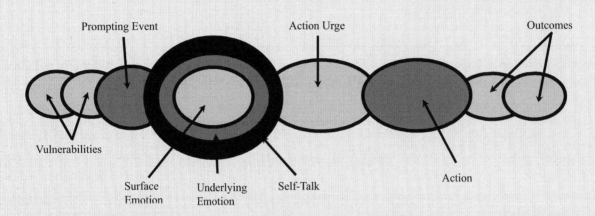

Describe your vulnerabilities:

Describe the prompting event (what set off the action?):

Describe your emotion on the surface (the one mostly easily noticed):

Describe any underlying emotions (the ones hidden underneath):

Describe your self-talk:

Describe the action urge:

Describe the action:

Describe the outcomes:

NOW GO BACK AND FILL IN SKILLS TO USE NEXT TIME AT EACH STEP

BEHAVIOR CHANGE ANALYSIS: SHORT FORM

Name: Date:

What was the SIB/TIB? Who? What? Where? When?

What led up to the SIB/TIB? Give specifics of what made you vulnerable and each factor (e.g., feelings, thoughts, behaviors, sensations, situations) that came before the SIB/TIB?

What did you gain or expect to gain by making that choice? How did you think it might help or benefit you? Did it meet your needs?

What were the negative consequences of your choice for you and others?

What skills could you use to meet your needs more effectively next time (in the short term and long term)?

      Short-Term Plan:

      Long-Term Plan:

BEHAVIOR CHANGE ANALYSIS: LONG FORM

Purpose: To get your needs met in a more effective manner through problem-solving around Self-Injurious Behavior (SIB) and Therapy-Interfering Behavior (TIB).

Step 1: Describe the SIB/TIB.

What did you do?

How did you do it?

Where did you do it?

When did you do it?

Who else was involved?

Step 2: Identify what was going on in your life before the SIB/TIB.

What event set off the SIB/TIB?

What were the events leading up to the event that set off the SIB/TIB?

Which of the events leading up to the SIB/TIB were the most important?

What were you feeling prior to and during the SIB/TIB?

What were you thinking prior to and during the SIB/TIB?

What need(s) were you trying to meet?

At what point did you make your decision to use the SIB/TIB?

Step 3: Identify the consequences of the SIB/TIB.

How may you have benefited from the SIB/TIB (in the short term and long term)?

How may you have been hurt from the SIB/TIB (in the short tem and long term)?

What changes happened with the following (in the short term and long term):

Feelings:

Thoughts:

Physical sensations:

Behaviors:

Events around you:

The way others treat you:

Step 4: Identify what DBT skills you could use to be more effective in a similar situation. (Review steps 1, 2, and 3, and look for ways to insert DBT skills at each step and sub-step.)

What DBT skills could you have used or could use next time when similar events take place?

What consequences to the SIB/TIB might help you to control or avoid that behavior in the future?

How can you remove access to the SIB/TIB?

What else might you do to get your needs met in an effective way that would not hurt you, others, and/or your treatment?

Step 5: Summarize the problem-solving in Steps 1–4.

What were the most important events leading up to the SIB/TIB?

What was the SIB/TIB?

What were the consequences of the SIB/TIB?

What DBT skills can you use and at what stage could you use them to get your needs met more effectively when similar events happen?

What is the earliest point at which you could insert skills?

Step 6: Identify resources/assets you have to implement DBT skills instead of using SIB/TIB.

What resources/assets do you have available that will assist your DBT skills use?

Additional input from your therapist, group, or significant other(s):

Behavior Contracts

Behavior contracts increase accountability by specifically defining problem behaviors and consequences. These contracts are useful when routine interventions for disruptive behaviors have not worked and when these behaviors have been ongoing in nature.

It is helpful to get clients' team members onboard with a behavior contract and to frame it as an effort to get clients on track and progressing in therapy. Clients may experience behavior contracts as punishment. Remember to validate the experience *and* indicate that a client's accountability to a behavior contract is in his or her best interest. Holding clients accountable for difficult behaviors shows caring and respect.

Remember that clients rarely engage in problem behaviors all *of the time. Behavior contracts will be as successful as therapists' efforts to continuously look for and reinforce non-problematic behaviors. Trying to extinguish a difficult behavior without reinforcing other effective behaviors is unfair to clients and ineffective in therapy.*

Below is a general behavior contract as well as a GIVE contract for clients who struggle with respectful behaviors in program and/or in relationships.

BEHAVIOR CONTRACT

The following behaviors have become disruptive to your therapy, your group, or the clinic:

1.
2.
3.
4.

The purpose of this behavior contract is to help you change these difficult behaviors so you can reach your treatment goals.

These behaviors will result in homework and/or change analysis. If you engage in these behaviors, your therapist and/or group members will respectfully observe and describe their presence, and you will have an opportunity to redirect the behaviors and practice skills.

If you choose not to redirect the behavior or practice skills, you will be asked to leave for the day, and the session will be counted as an absence. The absence will count toward the attendance policy.

If you are asked to leave, you may be suspended pending a team meeting. The team meeting may involve further problem solving or a decision to discharge you with referrals.

As part of this contract, your therapist and/or group members agree to notice and reinforce your efforts, positive behaviors, and skill use.

Signed by client: _____ Date: _____

Signed by therapist: _____ Date: _____

Original to client; copy to client

GIVE Contract

- Due to ongoing interpersonal difficulties in group, your immediate focus in treatment will be to learn and use GIVE skills.
- Until you can demonstrate the consistent use of GIVE, you will be expected to be **G**enuine, **I**nterested, **V**alidating, and use an **E**asy Manner with others as your primary way of relating.
- During your interactions in the program, you are to focus on the validation and encouragement of others.
- Disrespect of your therapist(s) and program members will be addressed and not tolerated.
- You are to take responsibility for yourself and help others to see the positives in you.

If your therapist and/or program members decide that you are not following these expectations, then the following will occur during the course of a session:

- You will be given a warning on the first occurrence.
- You will be assigned a Change Analysis on the second occurrence. Your Change Analysis must focus on your behavior, not the behavior of others, and it must be completed prior to your return to the next session. Your Change Analysis will be reviewed by your therapist prior to your presenting it.
- You will be asked to leave on the third occurrence. The absence will be subject to attendance policy expectations.

     If you are clearly disrespectful at any time, you will be asked to leave group and assigned a Change Analysis. Again, the absence will be subject to attendance policy expectations.

As part of this contract, your therapist and/or group members agree to notice and reinforce your efforts, positive behaviors, and skill use.

Signed by client: _____ Date: _____

Signed by therapist: _____ Date: _____

Original to client; copy to chart

Phone Coaching

Standard DBT requires the individual therapist to provide phone coaching availability to clients 24 hours a day, 7 days week. In standard DBT, this availability is balanced with limits, meaning that contingencies are established that keep clients from pushing the boundaries of therapists. If clients call too much or too often, it is treated as TIB. Therapists who do not observe limits with phone coaching might be practicing obtuse and unskillful limits or boundaries.

Phone coaching 24/7 is *not* proven to be a necessary component of effective DBT treatment. In fact, dialectical therapists find that there are both upsides and downsides to this level of availability.

Clients who do not have therapists with 24/7 availability learn that most life problems do not have immediate support and solutions and therefore practice their Distress Tolerance skills. These clients learn to rely on skills and other people in their support networks and to access support proactively with the knowledge that there are times when phone coaching is not available.

Therapists who choose to set limits on their availability model effective self-care and limits. They also teach clients about individual differences with boundaries.

All therapists who provide phone coaching (whether it is 24/7 or following an adapted plan) need to establish expectations for phone coaching up front. See the following for phone coaching expectations that can be applied across settings.

The primary function of phone coaching is to help clients generalize skills to everyday life between sessions. To meet this function, keep coaching calls brief and focused on skills; do not participate in "venting" calls or calls that turn into therapy sessions. In addition to phone coaching, and perhaps as a substitute, the use of the Skills Generalization Form is recommended.

Last, clients are not allowed to use phone coaching for 24 hours after the use of SIB or TIB to avoid the unintentional reinforcement of those behaviors. Clients are expected to call *before* acting on urges. If clients are reliant on your phone contact to stay out of danger and stay alive, they need a higher level of care.

PHONE COACHING EXPECTATIONS

Phone coaching is available to help you practice skills between sessions. Please follow these expectations:

- Phone coaching is for the generalization of skills.
- I cannot use phone coaching for 24 hours after I have engaged in SIB or TIB. I am expected to call *before* acting on urges.
- A phone coaching worksheet must be completed before the call.
- Phone coaching will focus on skills and not be therapy oriented.
- Phone coaching will be limited to 3 to 5 minutes.
- Not respecting the limits of phone coaching will be treated as TIB.
- Phone coaching availability and limits are established and negotiated up front by therapists and clients.

My therapist's availability, limits, and rules for phone coaching:

Signed by client: _____ Date: _____

Signed by therapist: _____ Date: _____

Original to client; copy to chart

203

PHONE COACHING WORKSHEET

Please complete this worksheet prior to calling for coaching.

Describe the problem or difficulty:

Describe the skills you have already used:

Describe what specific skills you need help with:

Describe what other skills or supports you can use if your therapist is not immediately available:

Specific Expectations:
- The call will focus on skills and last no more than 5 minutes.
- I will be willing to be coached and practice the specific skills.
- I will be respectful of my therapist's availability and limits.
- I understand that I will be hospitalized if I am unclear about safety issues.

SKILLS GENERALIZATION PLAN

Use to supplement or replace phone coaching.

Name:

Crisis Behavior:

List situational factors, feelings, thoughts, physical sensations, and behaviors typically associated with the crisis at each level of intensity.

0: No Crisis

Typical situational factors:

Typical feelings:

Typical thoughts:

Typical physical sensations:

Typical behaviors:

Skills in use:

1–2: Early Warning Signs

Typical situational factors:

Typical feelings:

Typical thoughts:

Typical physical sensations:

Typical behaviors:

Skills to use:

3–4: Some Distress

Typical situational factors:

Typical feelings:

Typical thoughts:

Typical physical sensations:

Typical behaviors:

Skills to use:

5–6: Increased Distress

Typical situational factors:

Typical feelings:

Typical thoughts:

Typical physical sensations:

Typical behaviors:

Skills to use:

7–8: Intense Distress

Typical situational factors:

Typical feelings:

Typical thoughts:

Typical physical sensations:

Typical behaviors:

Skills to use:

9–10: Crisis Point

Typical situational factors:

Typical feelings:

Typical thoughts:

Typical physical sensations:

Typical behaviors:

Skills to use:

Diagnoses and Symptoms:

Medications:

1.   Dosage:

2.   Dosage:

3.   Dosage:

4.   Dosage:

5.   Dosage:

6.   Dosage:

7.   Dosage:

Medical Alerts:

Contacts:

List people to call for support (family, friends, and team members to contact in the event of crisis):

Family members: Phone number(s):

Friends: Phone number(s):

Therapist: Phone number:

Psychiatrist: Phone number:

Case Manager: Phone number:

Other: Phone number:

Other: Phone number:

In Case of Emergency:

Call 911 or go to your nearest emergency room.

Program Graduations and Transitions

The reality of most programs is that clients can only be seen for a finite period of time within respective levels of care. Program graduations recognize clients who have met certain benchmarks and goals that signal the transition from your program to a lower level of care. Particular benchmarks and goals will be unique to your population and program and should be decided carefully with the clinical expertise of your therapists. The example given here might apply to an intensive program. In addition to these criteria, clinically significant change as measured by an outcome measure may be important to determine a transition to a lower level of care (i.e., less intensive treatment or discharge).

Not all clients graduate, and some clients will simply transition to other providers or to the community. Their hard work and accomplishments can still be recognized. Many people attend college classes, but not everyone completes a degree and graduates. Similarly, not all clients may meet your program's graduation standards, but the experience can still be valuable.

Client graduations and transitions require careful thought and planning to make sure therapeutic gains are consolidated and to minimize relapse. As with the entire course of DBT treatment, remember to sufficiently structure graduations and transitions.

When clients have progressed and are ready to move on, recognize their hard work and create a ceremony around the change in treatment or greater movement into the community. In addition to the graduation examples given here, traditional relapse prevention plans can be useful.

GRADUATION CRITERIA FOR AN INTENSIVE PROGRAM

- Average distress levels on Diary Cards at 3/10 or below for at least 3 months

- No hospitalizations for a psychological reason for at least 6 months

- No suicidal behavior for at least 6 months

- No Self-Injurious Behavior (SIB) for at least 3 months

- No Therapy-Interfering Behavior (TIB) for at least 2 months

- Completion of revised Safety/Crisis Plan and Skills Generalization Plan

- Completion of Graduation/Transition Discharge Plan

- Clearly identified social support

- Agreed-on transition plan to another level of care or to structure in the community

Graduation Discharge Plan

Describe the DBT skills that help when you're doing well:

Describe the DBT skills that decrease vulnerability to intense emotions:

Describe the DBT skills that help when you are in distress:

Describe the DBT skills that help when you are in crisis:

Describe your barriers to using DBT skills and skills to address those barriers:

Describe the DBT skills that will help when you experience setbacks:

Describe how your life is different from when you started the DBT program:

Attach the following:
1. Revised Routine/Schedule
2. Revised Safety/Crisis Plan
3. Revised Skills Generalization Plan
4. Revised Life Vision
5. List of social support with phone numbers

Original to client; copy to chart

GRADUATION TASKS

Verify with your therapist(s) that you meet the objective criteria for graduation.

1. Negotiate a graduation date with your therapist(s) and group.

2. Complete the Graduation Discharge Plan.

3. Revise your Routine/Schedule, Safety/Crisis Plan, Skills Generalization Plan, and Life Vision at least 2 weeks prior to the graduation date.

4. Present the items in #2 and #3 to your therapist(s) and/or group at least 2 weeks prior to graduation (to incorporate feedback).

5. Discuss your graduation plans with therapist(s), psychiatrist, team members, family, friends, and other supports.

6. Plan a graduation ceremony with your therapist(s) and/or group.

7. Proactively discuss problems and barriers to graduation with your therapist(s) and/or group.

On Your Graduation Day:

- Have a summary of your progress to share with your group.

- Say your goodbyes to peers, staff, and others. Prepare something memorable to share with each group member. Expect to hear from your therapist(s) and each group member. Grateful acceptance of compliments and positives indicates that you are ready to graduate.

Consultation Group

Consultation group is an essential element of DBT and is a best practice regardless of therapy approach or model. The purpose of consultation is to enhance the motivation and skill of therapists so that clients can receive the best possible therapy.

Consultation group follows DBT philosophies, which include a nonjudgmental approach to clients and to each other so that members feel supported when discussing problems, mistakes, and clinical shortcomings. The recognition that we all need support and that we are all fallible is central to effective consultation. Members are expected to be *active*, *mindful*, and *involved*.

Active, supportive, and accountable consultation groups reduce therapist burnout and build effective therapeutic responses. This approach helps us minimize iatrogenic responses that complicate our clients' difficulties and cause setbacks. Some examples of iatrogenic behaviors include lack of structure and accountability, extreme responses (e.g., too nurturing versus too strict), and causing or participating in boundary violations.

Most consultation groups have weekly readings and homework to stay current with DBT teachings, philosophies, and related topics. Some time spent reviewing and expanding the approach helps prevent "drift," in which therapists move too far away from the core approach.

Consultation group members generally sign an agreement and may be prescribed DBT "treatment," such as being asked to use a certain skill or asked to complete a behavior Change Analysis.

Most consultation groups meet weekly for 90 minutes. If you have a DBT program, it is encouraged that you have a consultative milieu within your program and clinic in which therapists can consistently seek out support and guidance.

It could be argued that consultation group is one of the most effective aspects of DBT since it directly benefits the therapeutic alliance. If you are unable to find or create a DBT consultation group, seek consultation from someone who values your clients and their outcomes over proving that their model or approach is better than yours (and show similar respect).

CONSULTATION GROUP AGREEMENT

This consultation group is a collective of therapists and providers working together to benefit all of our clients. We meet weekly for 90 minutes, and members can also consult by phone and secure email between consultation groups. Participation in this consultation group follows these guidelines:

- Members agree to 90% attendance of all consultation group meetings.

- Consultation group members will maintain a Nonjudgmental Stance toward clients and each other. We understand that clients and therapists are doing the best they can and need to do better. To do better, we need the regular support and guidance of consultation group members.

- Consultation group members will follow basic DBT philosophies and balance validation and change strategies with each other.

- Consultation group members will be active and mindful, present on clients, and give feedback to each other. Feedback is reciprocal and involves validation, encouragement, and suggested interventions.

- Consultation group members will come prepared with cases and will have completed agreed-on readings, assignments, and homework.

- Consultation group members will promote DBT in a positive manner that respects other providers and approaches.

I agree to be accountable to myself, to the other consultation group members, and to my clients.

Signed by therapist: _____ Date: _____

Clinical Outcomes Measures

The evidence-based practice of DBT (and therapy in general) requires the collection of clinical outcomes. Clinical outcomes can be used to monitor and adjust therapy for each individual and assess the overall effectiveness of your DBT program or services.

Clinical outcomes demonstrate accountability to clients and other stakeholders. Successful outcomes give clients and their therapists' confidence in the services provided.

Do not be afraid of clinical outcomes. The information they give allows you to fine-tune individual goals and objectives and to make quality improvements in your programming. Investigate options that fit your unique populations and programming.

Following are some suggested outcome measures, behaviors to track, and resources to get you started. Visit the suggested websites for more comprehensive information, and/or consult with a professional with a competency in tracking outcomes for additional guidance.

- Comprehensive measures like the Symptom Checklist 90 (SCL-90), Brief Symptom Inventory (BSI), and the Treatment Outcome Package (TOP) track symptoms and functioning across multiple domains. These measures work well for heterogeneous populations. Administer these measures at intake, every 3 months, and at discharge or as otherwise indicated based on the needs of your population. The SCL-90 and BSI are available from Pearson Assessments at www.pearsonassessments.com, and the TOP is available from Behavioral Health Labs at www.bhealthlabs.com.

- Targeted and brief measures like the Beck Depression Inventory (BDI) and the Beck Anxiety Inventory (BAI) can be useful. The Beck inventories are available from Pearson Assessments at www.pearsonassessments.com. Other options include the Outcome Rating Scale (ORS), Session Rating Scale (SRS), and Group Session Rating Scale (GSRS). These measures give close to real-time feedback on clients' functioning and connection to treatment. The ORS, SRS, and GSRS are available at www.heartandsoulofchange.com.

- Data on hospitalization rates before, during, and after treatment for populations known to have frequent hospitalizations (e.g., those with Borderline Personality Disorder) can demonstrate stabilization at a lower level of care and cost savings. Record both number of hospitalizations and number of days in the hospital for each incident.

- Data on suicide attempts and Self-Injurious Behavior (SIB) rates before, during, and after treatment for populations known for these behaviors can demonstrate stabilization, safety, and, potentially, cost savings.

- Quantifiable data on functional improvements that demonstrate clinically significant change or progress can be useful. Examples include decreased rates of alcohol or drug use; decreased rates of any specifically defined behavior problem; and increases in activities of daily living (ADLs), work or school attendance and performance, social contacts, or any specifically defined positive behavior. Make sure to clearly define targets to measure and to get accurate baselines for comparisons.

Master Skills List

Life Vision (LV): To focus on the life you are working toward

MIDDLE Cs (MC): To use a system to resolve dialectic conflicts

Wise Mind (WM): To dialectically balance emotion and reason so you can respond rather than react

Observe (OB): To just notice experience

Describe (DE): To put words on experience

Participate (PA): To get into your experience

Nonjudgmental Stance (NJS): To not attach strong opinions or labels to experience

One-mindfulness (OM): To focus your attention on one thing

Effectiveness (EF): To focus on what works

Teflon® Mind (TM): To not let things "stick to" you

ACCEPTS

> **Activities (AC):** To keep busy and involved

> **Contributing (CON):** To do something for others

> **Comparisons (COM):** To see that others struggle too

> **Emotions (EM):** To do something that creates other emotions

> **Push Away (PA):** To shelve your problem for later

> **Thoughts (T):** To think about something other than your distress

> **Sensations (S):** To do something physically engaging

Self-Soothe (SS): To relax yourself through the senses

Urge Surfing (US): To ride the ebbs and flows of emotions and urges without reacting

Bridge Burning (BB): To remove the means to act on harmful urges

IMPROVE the Moment

> **Imagery (IM):** To relax or practice skills visually in your mind

> **Meaning (ME):** To find the "why" to tolerate a difficult time

Prayer (PR): To seek connection and guidance from a higher power

Relaxation (RE): To calm the mind and body

One Thing at a Time (OT): To focus on one thing when life is overwhelming

Vacation (V): To take a brief break

Encouragement (EN): To coach yourself with positive self-talk

Pros and Cons (P&C): To weigh the benefits and costs of a choice

Grounding Yourself (GY): To use OB and DE to come back to the here and now

Radical Acceptance (RA): To acknowledge "what is" to free yourself from suffering

Everyday Acceptance (EA): To accept daily inconveniences that occur in life

Willingness (WI): To remove barriers and do what works in a situation

SOLVED (SO): To apply a values-based system for solving a problem

PLEASED (PL): To use a system of self-care skills

Build Mastery (BM): To do things to help you feel competent and in control

Build Positive Experience (BPE): To seek out events that create positive feelings

Attend to Relationships (A2R): To connect with meaningful people in your life

Mood Momentum (MM): To perform balanced behaviors to maintain positive moods

Opposite to Emotion (O2E): To do the opposite of the action a negative emotion pulls you to perform

ROUTINE (RO): To use a system for developing routines and schedules that help build a satisfying life

BOUNDARY (BO): To use a system for observing limits and boundaries in your relationships

FAST (F): To use a system for acting in a way that builds your self-respect

GIVE (G): To use a system for acting in a way that builds and maintains relationships

VALIDATION (V): To nonjudgmentally acknowledge someone's experience

DEAR MAN (DM): To use a system for asserting yourself, saying no, or setting a boundary

REASON (RE): To apply a system for shifting thoughts when needed

Source Citations for Modules and Skills

Life Vision (Pederson, 2011)

Dialectics Module (Pederson, 2011)

MIDDLE Cs (Pederson, 2011)

Mindfulness Module (Linehan, 1993b)

Wise Mind (Linehan, 1993b)

What Skills (Linehan, 1993b)

How Skills (Linehan, 1993b).

Teflon® Mind (Teflon is registered trademark of DuPont)

Distress Tolerance Module (Linehan, 1993b)

ACCEPTS (Linehan, 1993b)

Self-Soothe (Linehan, 1993b; expanded by Pederson, 2011)

Urge Surfing (similar to Ride the Wave, Moonshine, 2008)

Bridge Burning (Linehan, unpublished)

IMPROVE the Moment (Linehan, 1993b)

Pros and Cons (Linehan, 1993b)

Grounding Yourself (Pederson, 2011)

Radical Acceptance (Linehan, 1993b)

Everyday Acceptance (Pederson, 2011)

Willingness (Linehan, 1993b)

Problem Solving Module (Pederson, 2011)

SOLVED (Pederson, 2011)

Emotion Regulation Module (Linehan, 1993b)

PLEASE/PLEASED (Linehan, 1993b/adapted by Pederson, 2011)

Build Positive Experience (Linehan, 1993b)

Attend to Relationships (Eboni Webb, unpublished)

Mood Momentum (Pederson, 2011)

Opposite to Emotion (Linehan, 1993b)

Building a Satisfying Life Module (Pederson, 2011)

ROUTINE (Pederson, 2011)

Everyday Care (Pederson, 2011)

Boundaries Module (Pederson, 2011)

BOUNDARY (Pederson, 2011)

Interpersonal Effectiveness Module (Linehan, 1993b)
FAST (Linehan, 1993b)
GIVE/GIVE (Linehan, 1993b; adapted by Pederson, 2011)
VALIDATION (source unknown; adapted by Pederson, 2011)
DEAR MAN (Linehan, 1993b)
Shifting Thoughts Module (Pederson, 2011)
REASON (Pederson, 2011)

Bibliography

Therapists can expand their scope and practice of DBT, Mindfulness, Evidence-Based Practice, and related topics with these resources.

American Psychological Association. (2005). *Report of the 2005 Presidential Task Force on evidence-based practice.* Retrieved 1-3-2010 from http://www.apa.org/practice/ebpreport.pdf.

Brach, T. (2003). Radical acceptance: *Embracing your life with the heart of a Buddha.* Bantam: New York.

Clarkin, J. F., Levy, K. N., Lenzenweger, M. F., & Kernberg, O. F. (2007). Evaluating three treatments for borderline personality disorder: A multiwave study. *The American Journal of Psychiatry, 164,* 922–928.

Dimeff, L. A., & Koerner, K. (2007). *Dialectical behavior therapy in clinical practice: Applications across disorders and settings.* Guildford Press: New York.

Duncan, B. (2010). *On becoming a better therapist.* American Psychological Association: Washington, D. C.

Duncan, B., Miller, S., Wampold, B., & Hubble, M. (2010). *The heart and soul of change: Delivering what works in therapy,* 2nd ed. American Psychological Association: Washington, D. C.

Emmons, H., & Kranz, R. (2006). *The chemistry of joy.* Fireside: New York.

Emmon, H. (2010). *The chemistry of calm.* Touchstone: New York.

Fruzetti, A. E., & Linehan, M. M. (2006). *The high-conflict couple: A dialectical behavior therapy guide to finding peace, intimacy, & validation.* New Harbinger Press: Oakland.

Hanh, T. N. (1976). *The miracle of mindfulness.* Beacon Press: Boston.

Hayes, S. C., Strosahl, K. D., & Houts, A. (Eds.) (1999). *A practical guide to acceptance and commitment therapy.* Springer: New York.

Kabat-Zinn, J. (1994). *Wherever you go there you are: Mindfulness mediations in everyday living. Hyperion:* New York.

Kabat-Zinn, J. (1990). *Full catastrophe living: Using the wisdom of your body and mind to face stress, pain, and illness.* Dell: New York.

Kübler-Ross, E. (2005) *On grief and grieving: Finding the meaning of grief through the five stages of loss.* Scribner: New York.

Linehan, M. M. (1993a). *Cognitive-behavioral treatment of borderline personality disorder.* Guilford Press: New York.

Linehan, M. M. (1993b). *Skills training manual for treating borderline personality disorder.* Guilford Press: New York.

Marra, T. (2004). *Depressed & anxious: The dialectical behavior therapy workbook for overcoming depression and anxiety.* New Harbinger Press: Oakland.

Marra, T. (2005). *Dialectical behavior therapy in private practice: A practical and comprehensive guide.* New Harbinger Press: Oakland.

Mason, P. T. (1998). *Stop walking on eggshells.* New Harbinger: Oakland.

McKay, M., Wood, J. C., & Brantley, J. (2007) The dialectical behavior therapy skills workbook: *Practical DBT exercises for learning mindfulness, interpersonal effectiveness, emotion regulation & distress tolerance.* New Harbinger Press: Oakland.

Miller, A. L., Rathus, J. H., & Linehan, M. M. (2006). *Dialectical behavior therapy with suicidal adolescents.* Guilford Press: New York.

Moffitt, P. (2008). *Dancing with life: Buddhist insights for finding meaning and joy in the face of suffering.* Rodale: New York.

Moonshine, C. (2008). Acquiring competency & achieving proficiency with dialectical behavior therapy: Volume I – The clinician's guidebook. PESI: Eau Claire.

Moonshine, C. (2008). *Acquiring competency & achieving proficiency with dialectical behavior therapy: Volume II – The worksheets.* PESI: Eau Claire.

Nelson, W. (2006). *The tao of Willie: A guide to the happiness in your heart.* Gotham Books: New York.

Prochaska, J. O., Norcross, J., & DiClemente, C. (2007). *Changing for good: A revolutionary six-stage program for overcoming bad habits and moving your life positively forward.* Harper Collins: New York.

Spradlin, S. E. (2003). *Don't let your emotions run your life: How dialectical behavior therapy can put you in control.* New Harbinger Press: Oakland.

Wampold, B. E. (2001). *The Great Psychotherapy Debate: Models, Methods, and Findings.* Lawrence Erlbaum Associates: New Jersey.

Weinberg, I., Ronningstam, E., Goldblatt, M.J., Schechter, M., & Maltsberger, J.T. (2011). Common Factors in Empirically Supported Treatments of Borderline Personality Disorder. *Current Psychiatry Reports*, 13:60–68

Webb, C. A., DeRubeis, R. J., & Barber, J. P. (2010). Therapist adherence/competence and treatment outcome: A meta-analytic review. *Journal of Consulting and Clinical Psychology*, *78*(2), 200–211.

Other Resources

Dialectical Behavior Therapy Association (DBTA): www.pesi.com/dbta. This association provides a community for those interested in DBT. Membership gains access to a DBT message board and quarterly newsletters with articles and insights related to DBT. Visit the website for more information.

Dialectical Behavior Therapy National Certification and Accreditation Association (DBTNCAA): www.dbtncaa.com. This organization certifies DBT providers and accredits DBT programs that demonstrate the evidence-based practice of DBT. Visit their website for more information on these and other services.

Mental Health Systems, PC: www.mhs-pc.com. This private company has specialized in DBT services since 2002. Consultation and training on the DBT approach are available from Certified Dialectical Behavior Therapists. Visit their website for more information.

Made in the USA
San Bernardino, CA
21 November 2013